JONNY BAIRSTOW

& DUNCAN HAMILTON

A CLEAR BLUE SKY

To Hen
P.T.O.
Best Wishes

HarperCollins*Publishers*

HarperCollins*Publishers*
1 London Bridge Street
London SE1 9GF

www.harpercollins.co.uk

First published by HarperCollins 2017

1 3 5 7 9 10 8 6 4 2

All images © the author except: page 15 © Glyn Kirk/AFP/Getty Images;
page 132 © Adrian Murrell/Allsport UK/Getty Images; page 171 ©Adrian
Murrell/Allsport UK/Getty Images; page 190 © Ken Kelly/Popperfoto/
Getty Images; page 200 © Reuters/Philip Brown; page 210 © Adrian
Murrell/Allsport UK/Getty Images; page 241 © Adrian Murrell/Allsport
UK/Getty Images; page 245 © Bob Thomas/Getty Images; page 258
© Richard Heathcote/Getty Images; page 286 © Lindsey Parnaby/AFP/
Getty Images; page 297 © Julian Finney/Getty Images

A catalogue record of this book is
available from the British Library

HB ISBN 978-0-00-823267-2
PB ISBN 978-0-00-823268-9

Printed and bound in Great Britain by
CPI Group (UK) Ltd, Croydon

MIX
Paper from
responsible sources
FSC www.fsc.org **FSC C007454**

This book is produced from independently certified FSC paper
to ensure responsible forest management

For more information visit: www.harpercollins.co.uk/green

To Mum, Dad and Boo

CONTENTS

CONTENTS

EVERYTHING I'VE EVER STRIVED FOR, EVERYTHING I'VE EVER DONE

Cape Town, 3 January 2016

I'VE BEEN BATTING for more than three and a half hours. I've faced 160 balls. I'm on 99 – a nudge, a nick, a heartbeat away from my first Test century.

Just one more run …

This South African afternoon is heavy with a dry heat. The sky, shining without clouds, is as bright as the blue in a child's paint box, and the glare makes everything around me seem profoundly sharper: the sweep of a full, noisy ground, the purple-grey outline of Table Mountain and the jagged-ness of Devil's Peak, and even the vivid emerald of the outfield. In my head I'm talking all the time. I'm reminding myself, as I always do, of the simple things that are so damned difficult to get right. Stay focused. Appear calm, almost nonchalant. Don't let the bowlers get on top. And don't, on any account, show a sign of apprehension.

Between deliveries I've occasionally drifted out of my crease and patted down or brushed away some imaginary speck of dirt simply because I wanted something to do, something to keep me busy and alert. Or I've occupied myself in other ways: twirling my bat in my hand, tugging at my shirt and readjusting my helmet. These small tics are displacement, each designed to banish the sort of thoughts that can gremlin the mind. When you're so close to a hundred, it's easy to lose concentration. Your mind can go slack, wandering off abstractedly. Then the hard, sweaty graft that's gone before is undone in a nanosecond. So I have to stay in the moment. I mustn't get ahead of myself. I can't afford to think about the relief I'll feel when this is over and gone, already part of my statistical record. I can't afford to think about how handsome my name, illuminated on the scoreboard in big capital letters, will look with three figures beside it. And I can't afford to think about what the century will mean, professionally as well as personally. Most of all, I mustn't dwell on how I will feel or how I will celebrate in the middle. Or how my mum Janet and my sister Becky, who are sitting near the pavilion, will feel and celebrate too. Or how proud I will make them – this week of all weeks.

IN TWO DAYS' time it will be the family's black anniversary: the date of my dad's death in 1998. How quickly that always seems to come around. We mark it only among ourselves, and we do so very quietly, remembering the best of him rather than the tragedy of that day. New Year creeps up like a forewarning, and we get ourselves ready for the anniversary in our different ways. They say that for sorrow there is no remedy except time. Every turn of the calendar puts more distance between us and the raw pain of the event, but even a couple of decades on it scarcely lessens the degree of it. A stab of that pain always comes back.

When my dad died, taking his own life, I was eight years old. Becky, who everyone knows as Boo, was seven. My mum had cancer, the first of two bouts of the disease that she's fought and beaten. In that dark time – the worst imaginable – the three of us held tight to one another like survivors of a shipwreck. It was our only way to get through it. Our house, like our lives, seemed bare and empty and quiet, and our grief seemed inconsolable. We were hollowed out. But we had each other then – and we have each other still – and slowly we learnt to live without him. We came to accept his death, even though we don't understand it now any more than we did then.

Everyone believes their family is special. Mine just *is*. It isn't only about love. It's also about understanding and trust, support and the empathy between us. Because of what happened, and the way in which we coped with it, the three of us are as close as it's possible to be, our bond unbreakable.

I got a lot more genetically from my dad than my red hair. I got his eye for a ball. Early on I think he realised it or at least suspected that I could be a prodigy of sorts. Were he alive, or if he could come back to us for just one day – and how many occasions have I thought about *that* scenario? – I don't think he'd be too surprised to discover that I'm playing for Yorkshire and England. I bet he'd just give a nod and a knowing smile and say he expected nothing less from me.

When I was the smallest of small boys, a mere lick of a thing, I liked to play pool. My dad and I were once in a pub in North Yorkshire, one of those olde worlde places with low black beams and horse brasses. He had his pint. I had my apple juice. I couldn't have been more than six years old, possibly even a little younger. The two of us were at the table when a cycling club came in, wanting to play too. I have an inkling that there were five of them. My dad bet – a fiver, I think – that I could take on and whip the lot of them single-handed. The cyclists couldn't have been more incredulous if my dad had claimed to own a dog that could sing and dance. I was so short that I had to stand on a stool to make a shot. They looked at him as though he'd already drunk several beers too many. They looked at me – a wide-eyed, freckled lad – and accepted the wager without hesitation, certain of some easy cash. I took each of them to the cleaners, much to their mounting stupefaction and my dad's immense satisfaction. I know he wouldn't have made the bet if he hadn't thought I would win it; losing would have embarrassed both of us. So he must have thought his sporting streak was in me too.

If only I could ask him ...

He taught me how to hold a cricket bat. 'Pick it up like an axe,' he'd say. 'Grip it as though you're about to chop wood.' In knockabout games in our back garden, and especially on beaches as far flung as Barbados and Scarborough, he'd encourage me to give the ball a good tonk for the sheer joy of it. I'd swing my spindle-thin arms at a delivery, trying to

belt a huge six to impress him. I'd use one of his old bats – a V500 Slazenger – which he'd sawn down to my size. I kept that bat close to me, almost sleeping with it.

I'd tag along wherever he coached or turned out in charity matches, his first-class career already over by then. No question about it: my relationship with cricket began with my dad – and also because of him.

A lot of people, especially those who, like him, belong to the generation that grew up in the 1960s, still see me first and foremost as the son of my father. They always will, I guess. That's because the man who was plain Dad to me, a pal to be trailed after everywhere, was to everyone else David Bairstow, the Yorkshire cricket legend: a wicketkeeper and, for a while, captain emblematic of the county's traditions and passion for the game. Such public recognition meant there was no privacy in death for him, and consequently no privacy for us, either. Instead, there were front-page headlines, inky black and two inches high, a swarm of reporters and photographers standing at our gate, and television cameras at both his funeral and his memorial service.

Given the amount of publicity his death attracted, and bearing in mind the years that have passed, what I'm about to say seems impossible to believe but is perfectly true. Complete strangers, clearly fervent admirers with fond memories to share, will often come up and say to me casually, 'So how's your dad, then?' Some will launch into an anecdote about him and finish it before I have the chance to tell them that he died a while back (I don't usually elaborate about the details unless asked). Afterwards, they'll mumble 'sorry' and look a little self-conscious, as if not knowing is something to be ashamed about, which emphatically it isn't. Not for me. In reply I'll say 'no problem' and sincerely mean it because my dad had clearly touched their lives, even if only fleetingly, and left them a memory cherishable enough to speak out loud. It's proof, if I needed more of it, of how much he was admired.

How I wish he'd known that …

Others – and this may be even harder to believe – get confused and call me 'David', as though my dad's career at Headingley, which properly started in 1970, and my own, which began there almost four decades later, are somehow one and the same. I've got used to this. I've been answering questions about my dad ever since I learnt to talk. When your surname is Bairstow and you play in Yorkshire at any level, it's impossible to be anonymous – especially with a conspicuous mop of red hair.

At first my mum was a little wary about my ambition to become a cricketer. She was concerned in a protective way about the comparisons that she knew would be made straight away between my dad and me. About how I approached and played the game. About my character and his own. About how much I walked and spoke like him too. She worried that there'd be too much hassle and too much pressure placed on me because of it, but she kept all that to herself and never – not once – tried to steer me down a different path.

Since I knew comparisons were unavoidable, I prepared myself for them, even for the grumbling I expected to over-hear at some point, such as 'he's not a patch on his old man, is he?' or 'his dad would have caught that' or 'his dad would have knocked that ball into next week'. My mum, who is so level-headed, has always said that 'you can only be yourself

… there's no point in trying to be anything else', a slice of practical philosophy that I've carried around with me. I've drawn so much strength from what she says and the example she constantly sets. 'Extraordinary' is too feebly weak a word to fully do her justice. I could say she's one in a million, but the truth is that she's rarer even than that – much rarer, in fact.

We live our lives forwards, but only understand them backwards. Everything usually takes a firm shape and makes sense only in retrospect. There are still stages in life when you gaze around and say to yourself: How did I get here? Today at Newland's, on the brink of this hundred, is one of them for me. But the difference is *I know*.

I know how I jumped from school to club and then from club to Yorkshire's academy. *I know* how I got from the second XI into the County Championship side. And *I know* how I became an England player.

I've always tried to honour my dad and what he did for Yorkshire, which for him frequently meant putting the county's cause before his own. But my late boyhood, my early teens and then my adolescence were full of net sessions and practice drills he never witnessed, ups and downs he never knew about and matches he never saw. My mum was always there. So was Becky. Often, so were my maternal grandpa Colin, who took on the role of surrogate dad as well as his grandparent duties, and my grandma Joan. My grandpa died only seven months ago. I'm still grieving for him; something in me always will. We travelled en bloc, inseparable as a family. Reflecting on it all now, *I know* categorically that I wouldn't have come close to a career in cricket without them. In particular I've got to where I am because of my mum and Becky. That's why everything I've ever strived for – and everything I've achieved – has been done for them. I've wanted to look after them. I've wanted to repay them for their backing, their constant belief, even their gentle but persistent nagging of me sometimes.

Now I want to score this century for them too.

If I get it, there'll be tears shed later on from each of us. We'll look at one another, and shared memories of the past will make words superfluous.

Just one more run …

THERE'D BE AN odd irony about this century, a couple of small details that will make it seem as though everything about it was somehow preordained.

Perhaps so.

Batting is a tightrope walk, and it's always the precarious next step that bothers you. At the crease, you're secure only in the ball you've just faced. It's gone and done with, and can't get you out. But however well you've coped with it – you've picked the spin or read the late swing, you've pulled the bat away from something steeply rising or you've brilliantly clobbered a delivery on the up through extra cover – is then irrelevant. What matters is only the battle of the next ball. The nearer you get to a milestone score, especially a hundred, the more you can struggle. You have to handle the sense of anticipation in the crowd and also the expectation you begin to heap on yourself. The impulse to rush towards your hundred is perfectly natural and very human. There's a desire to get there quickly, so the accomplishment is already behind you. You can end up doing something rash. Or you can find the process debilitating and a torture. Some batsmen call it The Demon on Your Shoulder. Others call it The Joker or The Grudge. You suffer a kind of paralysis because of it. I know that from experience.

I've been in the 90s once before for England. That was against South Africa too; at Lord's, of all places, where to appear on the honours board is a kind of cricketing ennoblement. It was only my fourth Test. I'd made just 38 runs from four innings in the series against the West Indies at the start of the same summer. I was out of the side for the beginning of the series against South Africa to no one's surprise – including my own, really.

You probably won't remember why I found myself unexpectedly at Lord's, facing a pace attack of Morne Morkel, Vernon Philander and Dale Steyn. It was because of what *Wisden* euphemistically called 'textual impropriety'. Kevin Pietersen was dropped after allegations that he'd sent disparaging text messages about Andrew Strauss to some of the South African side during the Test at Headingley. It took some guts to axe KP; he'd scored a blazing 149 there, every stroke emphasising sublime, savage power. It also took some guts to bring me in as his replacement so quickly after I'd been dropped. The response, from commentators and critics alike, hovered between the sceptical and the scathing.

Against the West Indies, I'd had problems handling the short ball. The media saw me as a lame duck. The consensus was that the speed of Morkel, Philander and Steyn – fiercer collectively than anything I'd come across before – would wreck me. I'd be sliced and diced every which way, they said. My technique was microscopically picked apart. My temperament was picked apart too, as though I was on a psychiatrist's couch. The chief complaints against me – in no particular order – were:

That I wouldn't cope with the bouncer.
That I wouldn't cope with the occasion.
That I wouldn't cope, full stop.

Morkel, it was prophesied, would be my bête noire. He's nearly six-foot-six tall and he has such long arms. If he held them outstretched, he'd present a passable imitation of *The Angel of the North*. This means every delivery comes at you like something falling off a church steeple. Most batsmen wouldn't relish facing him if he had a Granny Smith in his hand, let alone a shiny, hard-seamed Duke.

I'd got to know and like Morkel when he ever-so-briefly played for Yorkshire at the beginning of the 2008 season. My mum is the club's Cricket Administrator and she liaises with the players, making sure those from overseas settle in. She cooked dinner for Morkel at our home and took care of him. He calls her 'my Yorkshire mum'. Without the ball in his hand he's a kindly, gentle man. With it, he's more than a nuisance. Even in the nets, off a shortened run, he was fast enough to make most of his contemporaries look merely 'nippy'.

In the swirl of controversy around KP, the build-up to the Test became weirdly askew; it was all about the man who wasn't there. The furious saga about his mobile phone, what was or wasn't said on it and whether the words constituted innocuous 'banter' or not, became a pitched battle. The claims and counter-claims and the accusations and denials swallowed up acres of newsprint and hours of TV, and provoked a blizzard of social-media comment, a lot of it X-rated. I was portrayed as an unfortunate sap, obliged to take on the impossible job of replacing one of the best batsmen on God's earth. It was assumed I'd turn up, barely trouble the scorers and seldom be heard of again. Since I was expected to fail, the pressure on me wasn't anything like the pressure on Strauss – about to play his hundredth and last Test – and England's coach, Andy Flower, both of whom had demonstrated such a fabulous faith in my abilities, an act for which I'll be eternally thankful. If I cocked up, the flak would be flying at them first and me second.

That Test, the final of the series, wasn't just about bragging rights and kudos either. We were one down and attempting to cling on to our status as the top Test nation. But, when I came in, we were 54 for four and staring calamity in the face. Morkel was ripping it in at almost 90 miles an hour. He welcomed me with a short leg and a leg gully, which was hardly a code in need of cracking about the length and line of his attack. I'd prepared for it. I'd been in the nets, where our batting coaches, Graham Gooch and Graham Thorpe, had for hours flung short balls at me from a dog stick. I also wore for the first time cricket's equivalent of a bullet-proof vest – a chest pad.

The third ball Morkel bowled was six inches short of a length and jumped at me like fat spitting from a pan. I bent down a little and yanked my head out of its flight-path. There were a few more like this – or of a similar variety, some spearing towards my ribcage – before he switched to around the wicket, tilting the angle and making it sharper. When you're being peppered like this, you're always waiting

for the inevitable – the yorker that's fast enough to turn your toes to pulp or send a stump cartwheeling. It came, and I was ready for it. I got into position and clipped the thing away for four, which was a turning point psychologically. I'd stood up to Morkel, and now he – along with Steyn and Philander – realised I wasn't a soft touch. I eased to 50 without much bother. I eased to 90 in the same way. I imagine that whoever's responsible for putting the names on that oak honours' board in the Lord's dressing room was preparing to stencil my own there. Then I got stuck, as if in quicksand. I inexplicably couldn't get the ball away.

After every innings you replay the chances you missed: the stray delivery on your pads that you should have flicked to the boundary; the half-volley that you curse yourself for mishitting; the short ball you didn't punish. In 40 minutes, I made only one run. On 95, I failed to score for 14 balls. I had about four chances to regain my authority and my momentum and claim that century. I wasn't able to take any of them. Finally, out of desperation, I spotted what I thought was the perfect opportunity to on-drive Morkel to the fence. So I went for it. Rather than the romantic sound of willow on leather, I heard the terrible rattle of leather on ash as the bails went for a little dance. I'd played around the delivery.

The ovation I got for an innings-saving score – and then for a 41-ball fifty when batting again – was wonderful music, but not entirely consoling. Nor were the complimentary critiques of each knock. My dad was mentioned. I'd done him proud, they said. I'd evoked his spirit and shown the guts and gusto that, time and again, had hallmarked his own cricket. But we lost the Test, lost the series, lost our number one ranking and Strauss retired as a consequence. Someone once said that the most beautiful rebuke you can ever utter is 'I told you so'. My performance would have allowed me to use it, but I didn't. I was too busy kicking myself rotten for not getting the hundred. That was nearly four years ago, which is a lifetime in sport, a profession where most careers constitute not much more than a brief flash of time compared with the life that comes after them.

But Lord's is only one reason why it would be fitting to get my Test first century now, exacting a kind of revenge against South Africa in the process. On England's tour here, exactly six years ago, I was a spectator. I sat in an executive box, staring down the line of the stumps. That day I let my eyes roll right across Newlands, one of the great theatres of cricket. It's the sort of place where you'd gladly play every week purely for the picturesque sight of it. I gathered in every square foot of the ground, which was cast in hot sun and dark shadow. Two South Africans scored centuries in a game that was dramatically drawn in the last over of the last day: Jacques Kallis got one in the first innings; Graeme Smith got another in the second. Watching them in that Test, I quietly resolved – telling no one about it – to come back here and make a century too.

Just one more run …

I CAN SEE the executive box where my younger self sat, and I wonder who is sitting in it today. Whoever has the privilege will envy me the plumb position I've had during one of the best innings I've ever seen. When I came in, we were 223 for five, and Ben Stokes was on 24, just warming up. We ended the first day on 315: him on 74, me on 39. He's now on double Nelson – 222 – and the two of us, the ginger twins, have taken the score on to 538. Talk about being in the groove. In the past two and a half hours he's dismantled the South African attack nut and bolt. He's striking the ball so hard that I wouldn't be surprised to see it spontaneously combust. The way he's seeing it, bigger than a party balloon, and the way he's hitting it, each attacking stroke like a booming detonation, he could probably have reached his first century using one of the stumps. He's walloped everything everywhere, and none of the bowlers is escaping punishment. No matter how they bowl to him, or where the ball lands, he seems to know what's coming at him, as if he's developed a sixth sense. It's been a prolonged burst of clean, pyrotechnical hitting. The ball is travelling so far that South Africa might be better off posting a couple of fielders on Table Mountain.

Our partnership has been an unselfish one. I've known Stokesy for eleven and a half years, ever since we played against one another in an under-15 County Cup match at Sowerby, a ground ringed by tall heavy trees, plain houses and hills topped with a row of unlovely electric pylons. I was 15. He was a fortnight shy of his 14th birthday. Imagine if someone from the future had turned up then, tapped us both on the shoulder and said: 'One day, lads, the two of you will swap this for Cape Town.' We'd have dismissed the remark as insane. Stokesy's dad was also a pro sportsman, a New Zealand rugby league international and then a coach in England. So he knows what it's like to grow up with a name that gets recognised. He knows, too, that reaching this century for me will be about more than the landmark of the score itself; that the past as much as the present will be entwined within it.

In between overs we come together and touch gloves. Denis Compton, whose day was a few ice ages before my own, would apparently cheerfully ask his most frequent batting partners which club or bar the two of them might frequent later on that night. Or he'd tell them about his galli-vanting exploits during the evening before. What Stokesy and I say to one another isn't remotely as entertaining as that. None of our exchanges will make it into the *Oxford Dictionary of Quotations* either. We offer nothing more than 'well done, mate' or 'keep going' or 'you can do it'.

You have this dreamy image of reaching your first Test hundred with one of the showboat strokes – a ravishing drive through extra cover or something smacked along the ground straight past the bowler. But when you're almost there, right on top of a ton, you're grateful to get home any old how. Even the faintest of faint edges or something slightly streaky will do – an inside edge past leg stump and the wicketkeeper. Yes, I'd gladly take that.

I haven't tried to prove I can match Stokesy shot for shot. A year or two ago it would have been different. I would have impetuously tried to keep pace, getting myself caught up in the whirl of things and wanting to demonstrate that I'm no slouch either when it comes to finding the boundary. But I'm a more measured and mature batsman than I used to be; a bit older and a lot wiser than the bloke who got into a tangle and let Morne Morkel get the better of him in 2012.

At lunch I was on 95, which threw up one of those strange coincidences. I know it won't have gone unnoticed among the South Africans. Morkel in particular will have thought about Lord's – and he'll have known that I was thinking about it too. Because of that, I did something I wouldn't normally do. In the dressing room I didn't take off my pads or my box or my boots. I wanted, as much as I possibly could, to pretend the break wasn't happening. In the hubbub I sat largely in silence, left alone as I waited for the clock to tick around and send me back out again. I knew Morkel would be waiting for me; that he'd be thrown the ball again as soon as the afternoon session began. So it proved. He bowled tightly, forcing me to play five of his first six deliveries – all of them dots.

Sometimes you hit a shot that makes you feel it's going to be your day. It's something fluid and naturally stylish, taking no effort. You do it not only instinctively but also unconsciously, and you understand immediately afterwards, as you're still watching the ball sail away from you, that today everything is well-oiled and working solidly. The bat is a physical part of you. This happened to me after I went past fifty. It was an on drive against Morkel. The ball was fullish, not too dissimilar to the one that got me out at Lord's. I waited for it, got my head over it and then thumped it past him. I felt in charge then, and I still feel in charge now.

Just one more run …

SOUTH AFRICA HAVE taken off Morne Morkel and brought on Stiaan van Zyl, a batsman who can bowl. He's a bits and pieces medium pacer, called on only occasionally. He's less experienced in Tests than I am; he's taken only four wickets in nine appearances before this one. That said, one of his victims was Virat Kohli. And another – in the previous Test at Durban – was me. In the second innings, I was on 79 and eyeing a century the way I am today. But I was running out of partners and went back into my crease to crash the living daylights out of an ordinary delivery. I miscalculated. I didn't put enough juice into the shot and I holed out at long off, getting a rollicking for it later.

Van Zyl has been put on to remind me of Durban. To lull me into relaxing against him and committing another error. The difference between him and Morkel, who is fielding on the boundary, is as stark as the difference between a light breeze and a lashing wind. Van Zyl sends down innocuous-looking deliveries, the odd one drifting away or cutting back. I'm wary of him purely because of my score. To get from 95 to 99, I filched one single off Morkel and three off

Van Zyl. I'm still waiting for the unexpected from him. The Wonder Ball. Something he's hidden so far. Something that seems nothing in the air but is everything off the pitch – either dipping low, towards my bootstraps, or darting up, forcing me to fend it off.

Like Donald Bradman before him, Brian Lara said he didn't focus so much on the fielders as on the gaps between them. I'm checking and rechecking the set of the field, looking for the spaces too, so that I'll know with a nailed-on certainty where to send anything loose. South Africa are tinkering with the field. It's dragged in before minor adjustments are made – a yard here, a few paces there. It's an attempt to deprive me of a single and persuade me to hit over the top. This drawn-out process is also an attempt to niggle and make me feel nervous. It won't. I'm telling myself three things:

Patience … Patience … Patience.

The crowd is pent-up. There's cheering and hollering and chanting until just before the ball is bowled, when a silence engulfs the ground. It's as though everyone is holding their breath for me.

It's the fourth ball of the 118th over. It's the 161st ball of my innings.

Possibly the heat has wearied Van Zyl. Or possibly he is just a tad too eager to get at me, and the strenuous effort he puts into the delivery throws his stride out, leaving him fractionally off-balance. Whatever the reason, his arm gets dragged down just a sliver as he heaves his body into it. As a batsman, you're constantly dealing with the infinitesimal.

Judgements are made in millimetres and in microseconds. Get any calculation wrong, and you're likely to perish. Everything happens so quickly, the ball on top of you after a blur and a kerfuffle of movement. In the time it takes to blink you're working out speed, trajectory and direction. Even someone of Van Zyl's relatively sedate pace demands that. But I see this ball early. And, almost as soon as it leaves his hand, I know its length and line. I also know which stroke I'll play – a cut past backward point, a shot I've executed in games innumerable times and practised innumerable times more. My dad loved the cut. 'If they bowl short outside the off stump, it's bingo,' he used to say. This is bingo for me too. I go back and across my stumps, ever so slightly crouching. I'm in position, waiting for it before it arrives. This is my moment and I've come to meet it.

You know when you've hit a good shot. I use a bat that weighs 2 pounds and 9 ounces, and it makes a reassuringly solid sound when I connect properly. The ball pings off the middle. I start to run, but there's no need. It's going for four.

The 'YES' I scream in response is half roar, half rebel yell. It's loud enough for someone to hear it in Leeds. I'm still shouting it, and still wearing my helmet, when I lean back, arms outstretched. Then I yank my helmet off, kiss the badge on the front of it and hold my bat aloft. I tilt my head upwards. All I see is the unblemished arch of the sky, clearer and bluer than ever. All I hear is the crowd – the clapping, the cheers, the thunder of voices. What I feel is absolute relief and the profoundest joy. I am experiencing what I can only describe as the sense of complete fulfilment, which is overwhelming me.

I'm so grateful to Ben Stokes. It's second nature to dash to your partner when he reaches a hundred, sharing the stage with him. Stokesy doesn't. He stands back, a spectator like everyone else, allowing me a minute alone. He *knows*. Finally, he throws one of those big, tattooed arms around me and says: 'Soak it up. Take it all in, mate.'

I do.

And what comes back, of course, crowding into my mind, is the past, which puts everything into context. My dad. My grandpa. My grandma. My mum. My sister. I could weep now. I could let the tears out, but I fight against them instead, closing my eyes to dam them up.

My dad always liked to know where my mum was sitting before he went in to bat. He drew comfort from the fact that she was there and giving her support – even when he couldn't see her distinctly. At the beginning of his innings he'd search for her from the crease and settled only when he'd fastened on to the approximate location or, better still, actually spotted her in a row, usually because of something she was wearing. I'm exactly the same. I'll always look in her direction, searching for her face among a thousand others.

My mum is sometimes unable to look when I bat; she might hide in a corridor when I get near a landmark score. I know she'll have braved this one out, but everyone is standing and applauding so I can't see her at first. I point with my bat towards where I know for certain she and Becky are sitting, a gesture for them alone.

Eventually the noise of the crowd dies away, and I think of starting my innings again. But first I take one last look at the sky. If heaven has a pub, I hope my dad is in it now. I hope he's ordering a pint to celebrate.

Then I hope he orders another.

CHAPTER 1

THE VIEW FROM THE VERANDA

FIRST, THE BARE, stark fact – the matter of public record.

My dad was only 46 years and 126 days old when he committed suicide. My mum, my sister Becky and I found him when we returned home at 8.30 p.m., which was one of those typically lampblack and cold January nights. He had hanged himself from the staircase.

Now, the speculation – the what ifs, the what-might-have-beens, the guesswork.

The great risk of being alive is always that something can happen to you – or to someone you dearly love – at any moment. I learnt that lesson on a Monday evening so ordinary that otherwise it would be indistinguishable from a thousand-and-one others. Everything seemed normal to me. They say that even the sensibilities of infants can pick up a minute shift of mood at home, alerting them when something is a little odd or off. I'd gone past the stage of infancy – I was a young child – but I'd registered nothing untoward. To me, my dad was just my dad, as ebullient and as energetic as ever. I never saw him down or doubtful, or fretful about either himself or our future. I had no inkling that anything was wrong. He didn't seem like a man full of distractions to me.

In the morning I said goodbye to him and walked to school with Becky, the Christmas holidays over and a new term beginning. In the early evening my mum took me to football training at Leeds United, bringing Becky too. That our lives changed irrevocably while the three of us were away seemed to me – then as well as now – inconceivable and incomprehensible.

The inquest into my dad's death, which I didn't attend, heard evidence about his mental state. That he'd been suffering from depression and stress. That he'd seen both his own doctor and a consultant psychiatrist because of it. That he'd experienced extreme mood swings, veering between the dramatically high and the dramatically low, leaving my mum unsure about 'which version of him would come through the door'. That he'd been for a drink at one of his favourite pubs a few hours before he died (though the toxicology report revealed no extravagant level of alcohol in his system). That he'd been concerned about my mum's health and the treatment she was undergoing for breast cancer, diagnosed less than three months before and far more aggressive than even she appreciated at the time. She'd undergone chemotherapy, radiotherapy and then chemotherapy again. She was wearing a wig because her hair had fallen out. I didn't know – but I learnt later – that the hospital became more concerned about my dad's emotional state than my mum's.

He was afraid she was going to die. He was also afraid of how he would cope – and what would happen to us – if she did.

Also, my dad had been particularly anxious about an impending court appearance to answer a drink-driving charge, which would certainly have meant the loss of his licence, a potentially grievous blow to his promotional and marketing business – and to our family finances. The incident precipitating it was an accident on a quiet country road the previous October. My dad was bringing me home from training at Leeds in his Volkswagen Scirocco. A car, coming in the opposite direction, dazzled him with its headlights, which were unusually bright. For a split second, my dad lost control of the wheel. We veered off the road, struck a slight bank and the car tipped over. The Scirocco ended up on its right side, leaving me on top of my dad.

Shoeless, and still wearing my football kit, I freed myself and then clambered over him, escaping through the back window. With only the odd cut and bruise, which was miraculous, I stood in the middle of the road and waited. The driver who'd blinded my dad hadn't stopped; he'd sped away, long gone and unidentifiable. A friend of mine, also on Leeds' books, was being taken home by his father. I flagged them down, and the police and an ambulance were called. That afternoon my dad had been at the funeral of a golfing buddy. Like everyone else, he'd gone to the wake afterwards. The police routinely brought out the breathalyser, finding him over the limit. I can't condone my dad's drink-driving, but the circumstances surrounding the case – the car responsible for it, the driver absconding afterwards without a care for our well-being, the fact that my dad hadn't been speeding – didn't seem to interest the police. I, the only other witness, wasn't even asked to give a statement. I am still livid about that.

The repercussions of the crash rippled out. My dad was mortified that he'd put me in danger, mulling over afterwards how much worse the crash could have been. It left him with a debilitating arm injury. His future in local cricket, and also the enormous pleasure he got from playing golf, were both jeopardised. His right arm and shoulder required an operation, and 16 pins and a plate were put in to support his joints, which brought him considerable pain during his ongoing recovery.

Fraught with worry as the court case loomed and his other problems accumulated, my dad had not only been drinking too much generally – and he accepted as much – but a few weeks earlier he had also swallowed an overdose of painkillers at home: the same painkillers that had been prescribed for his injuries. He described taking them as 'a cry for help'. My mum had for months urged him to go to a doctor and talk openly about his depression. Either he refused or, after giving in and going to an appointment, he threw up a smokescreen for the doctor's benefit. He pretended there wasn't anything wrong with him that wouldn't soon be shaken off. 'He and the doctor ended up talking mostly about sport,' my mum said.

The coroner was patient and sympathetic, aware of my dad's popularity and the accounts of him as a decent family man. He recorded an open verdict, as certain as he could be that my dad hadn't meant to die. He was making a further 'cry for help', and it had gone wrong in a way that he hadn't foreseen and didn't intend because his illness confused him and clouded his judgement. My dad, knowing that we were on our way home, thought we would rescue him, added the coroner. As it turned out, one small innocent delay after another – none of them anyone's fault – meant we arrived back half-an-hour later than we'd planned.

The coroner's concise, concluding sentence encapsulated the difficulty for those of us left behind looking for closure and searching for The Why behind his death.

'*I do not know what happened,*' the coroner said. '*He is the only one who did.*'

Though almost 20 years have passed, I'm no closer to an explanation for what happened, which makes it harder to accept. Why my dad decided to end his life, and why he did so that evening, is an unsolvable puzzle. There was no note to read, no definitive clue to discover. There were fragments, just bits and pieces of information, but putting them together to reconstruct his last months never created a coherent whole that made absolute sense and explained everything, especially about what he must have been thinking. No matter how hard I tried, from what I knew as I grew up or discovered subsequently, there were always gaping holes. Questions that can't be answered. Things that don't add up.

The truth is snagged somewhere in between them, caught in one of those places that's impossible to reach.

I live with that.

The following day was my mum's 42nd birthday. Only a few hours before he died my dad had gone to a nearby town and booked a celebratory meal for the two of them. He'd also booked a babysitter to look after Becky and me. That act makes what he did seem even more illogical to us than ever. So did something he said not long before. After a friend of his died, also committing suicide by hanging, he'd asked my mum, disbelievingly: 'Why on earth would anyone do that?'

I suppose I could track down everyone my dad saw or spoke with towards the end, but I'm sure doing so would produce only more contradictions, more confusion. For on the one hand he'd recently told a journalist friend, during a train journey to London, that he was in fine fettle and eager for 1998 to start. 'I'm at the top of my form,' he'd insisted. On the other, he'd told Mike Brearley, who had been his England captain, completely the opposite. 'He felt awful ... things were not good,' reported Brearley.

So, instead of certainties, there are only theories, and always will be. My mum believes there were 'small bereavements inside him', among them the loss of his cricket career, his search for something to replace it – which he never found – and also the death of his father. My dad was an only child. His father raised him all but alone after his mother abandoned the two of them. He was only three years old. My dad never saw his mother again, relying on his aunts to offer the maternal care every child needs. When, shortly before she died, his mother wrote and finally wanted to see him, my dad didn't want to meet her. He was still playing for Yorkshire then. 'She's known where I've been for the last thirty years and hasn't bothered to visit,' he told my mum. 'I don't want to hear from her now. It's too late.' My mum tried conciliation, telling him: 'There are always two sides to a story ... perhaps she'll explain why she left and why she hasn't been in touch since.' My dad wasn't interested. One of the most perplexing letters of condolence we received after my dad's death came with an Australian postmark. The writer, a complete stranger to us, asked my mum to pass on his sympathies to my dad's 'brother'. She wrote back explaining that, as far as she knew, my dad didn't have a brother. If he did, we still don't know anything about him.

Apart from the hurt and anger that her unexplained absence left simmering in him, perhaps my dad didn't want to see his mother again because doing so would have been a betrayal of his father. He was christened Leslie, but everyone called him Des after his own father – apart, of course, from my dad, who referred to him as 'Pops'. He was a smaller version of my dad with bow legs so pronounced that stopping a pig in a passage would have been difficult for him. He was born on the last day of 1916, the year in which the Battle of the Somme claimed more than a million casualties. Some of the killed, maimed and injured belonged to battalions made up of Bradford Pals, including members of the extended Bairstow family. He was given the middle name Somme because of it. He'd played cricket for Laisterdyke, both before and after the Second World War as a wicket-keeper, served overseas in the army and ended his working life in a chemical factory. He was an old-fashioned sort of gent, usually seen carrying a rolled-up newspaper. As a greeting back to anyone who said hello, he'd tap the top of his forehead with the newspaper, a show of northern politeness.

My dad adored his father. Early in his career he would often dedicate a catch, a stumping or an innings to him, telling reporters: 'Pops will be proud of that.' The two of them were good companions and each loved and felt indebted to the other. My dad kept a black-and-white photograph of his father in his wallet and put another much larger and colourised version of it on the wall at home. Every year, paying tribute to his father's military background, he'd wear his poppy proudly and we would attend the Remembrance Day service at Boroughbridge, the town closest to us.

My dad died almost to the day that his own father had died 16 years before. Was that a coincidence? I don't know; I never will.

Illness does its early work in secret, so another crucial aspect I don't know is when his own began. My dad once declared 'I love life'. For so long he gave every indication of doing that, making it impossible to pinpoint precisely when feeling a little down became melancholy and then tipped into an engulfing depression. My dad had suffered a succession of setbacks. He'd applied for the job as Yorkshire's Cricket Manager, believing he was the ideal candidate. He didn't get it. He considered standing for the committee until the prospect of success dimmed for him. He'd been doing occasional commentaries for the BBC, and listeners liked him, but a more permanent role went to someone else. He'd been steadily hunting down promotional work, which was becoming harder to get. He'd been running his own company, winning a contract to merchandise World Cup ties.

Life without cricket was initially harder for my dad than playing the game had ever been. He missed it, and also the adrenalin pump of a performance. He missed the crack and the camaraderie of the dressing room eight years after leaving it too. For two decades he'd got himself set for the glad rush of each new summer, and he sincerely believed he had a few more of them left in him. But, when he was 38, Yorkshire nudged him reluctantly into retirement before he was ready or properly prepared for it. He remained convinced, for at least a season or two afterwards, that he was still good enough for the County Championship team. He was almost waiting for Yorkshire to realise this and recall him, which in the beginning made it more difficult to settle into an alternative career. There is nothing he wouldn't have done for them. His roots were in Yorkshire cricket. So were his inspirations. And so was his identity, his sense of self.

My dad wore the White Rose on his sleeve, the county's emblem becoming his own. The county was bone and blood and breath to him. He once stood on top of the huge concrete marker post, emblazoned with that White Rose, which tells the traveller on the M62 where Lancashire ends and Yorkshire begins. He wore his full kit, and brandished a bat with his arms flung wide. This wasn't a pose. Nor was the beaming expression he wore put on for the sake of a good picture. My dad really did believe that Yorkshire was the epicentre of the world.

The Cricketer once ran a headline that said: 'Bairstow ready to shed tears for Yorkshire'. Shed tears he did – and plenty of them. I've reliably heard that he played every match for Yorkshire – even a friendly – as though it was a Test; and also that every defeat was a grievous wound to him. He once said: 'I took defeat quite badly. I tried not to show how much I cared to the others. More often than not I went for a long brisk walk on my own. I would march along, getting it out of my system ... I was better on my own.' He also admitted that there were 'times when I feel down, just like everyone else, and then I need others to pat me on the back, crack a joke or two and take the job that I normally do'.

One of his colleagues, John Hampshire, even wrote in my dad's benefit brochure that he was prone to 'fits of depression' when Yorkshire didn't perform – or when he didn't perform for them. 'When this man is down the whole world knows about it,' he added. After his death, the assessment was plucked out in isolation, over-analysed and misinterpreted. John, one of the nicest men I knew, was talking about the sad low of losing rather than highlighting the medical definition of clinical depression. For when my dad did have the condition, the evidence of how capably he concealed the fact – telling pretty white lies about it – was contained in the shock his suicide created.

A doctor can ask a patient who has a physical pain 'where does it hurt?' The patient will point to a specific spot. With a mental illness, it hurts everywhere. During the past decade in particular, we've only just begun to understand such a simple fact and take some long and welcome strides towards a more compassionate understanding of it. We've also developed an appreciation about the right and wrong ways of discussing and handling mental illness. The language we use when referring to depression has changed. Mercifully gone is the edge of mockery, condescension and flippancy that used to be commonplace. This change was slow in coming, and more change is still needed, but we've grown up and matured as a society, realising nowadays that no shame or stigma should ever be attached to the condition.

People in my dad's day, especially those associated with a macho sport, were wary at best and petrified at worst about coming forward and confessing to a problem. For a man, it wasn't manly, a situation that seems ridiculous to us now. You could be perceived as weak or written off as damaged goods. That is why my dad disguised his own depression with a façade in those conversations with his doctors. It was a convincing act in which he pretended to be himself, proving again that mental illness can be invisible to the naked eye when the sufferer never complains and presents a pasted-on smile to the world.

At Yorkshire, he'd been given two nicknames. The first was 'Stanley', after the Bradford-born writer Stan Barstow, author of *A Kind of Loving*, one of those popular kitchen-sink novels of the late 1950s and early 1960s. No one quibbled over the missing 'i'. The second, which he relished, was 'Bluey', the slang word Australians use for anyone with red hair. My dad also had eyes that were bright blue, so the name, which John Hampshire gave him, stuck. It fitted him as well as a handmade suit; 'Bluey Bairstow' rolled off the tongue. There was something breezy and high-spirited about it that matched his approach to the game as well as to life. 'After that,' my dad said, 'no friend ever called me David again – unless they were telling me off.'

However dreadful he surely felt inside during his bad days, I think my dad strove outwardly to be the Bluey every-one expected – confident, lively and always as full of bonho-mie as he could be. The copious newspaper reports of his death, each of the cuttings torn and yellow with age now, show how successfully he maintained the pretence. Fred Trueman found his suicide 'beyond belief'. Fooled like so many others, Brian Close thought my dad had been his 'normal self' when he last saw him only a few months before. Even his former teammate Phil Carrick, whose friendship with my dad almost went back to the time both of them were in short pants, was stupefied. 'I just can't take it in,' he said. Another long-standing friend, Michael Parkinson (now

Sir Parky), had latterly detected a certain 'sadness in him', but still couldn't credit what had happened. His reply, when hearing about my dad's suicide, was to dismiss the bringer of such awful news with the incredulous: 'Don't be daft. Not Bluey.'

Few knew my dad was sick, and fewer still knew the extent of that sickness, because he hid it far too well.

Torturing yourself with 'what if?' questions is pointless. No matter how long you dwell on them you only ever end up circling back to the spot where you started, absolutely no wiser. But you can't help asking them anyway. So I wonder whether, if modern attitudes had been prevalent back then, allowing my dad to be more open about his depression – making his cry for help more public – he would still be here with us …

Possibly.

ONCE A THING is known, it cannot be unknown – especially when you've seen it with your own eyes. But in the weeks, months and years that followed my dad's death, I tried to blot out the memory of how it happened as much as I could. In significant ways, I succeeded. Gone are the raw details of what I witnessed and also what was done and said in the immediate aftermath of it. Perhaps I was just too young to absorb them in the first place. Or perhaps trauma oblite-rated them, the mind deliberately wiping away in an act of self-protection what was too hurtful to bear. I can't tell you who among the three of us was first through our front door. I can't tell you how we got from our house to our neighbours, which is where we apparently went. But what remains – and always will for me, I think – is how I felt, then and for a long while later: vulnerable and afraid, the sense of disorientation and loss overwhelming. I learnt only retrospectively about the five stages of grief, but I experienced each of them to a different degree – especially the first, which is denial. I knew what death was, and I also knew categorically what it meant. Nonetheless there were times, particularly when I first woke up in the morning or returned to the house from somewhere, when I half-expected to find my dad still alive, smiling and sitting in his chair, exactly as I'd known him. Or I was sure I'd hear his car on the drive and his key turn in the lock. I'd see him framed in our wide front door, ready to pick me up in his big arms again for a hug; a hug so muscular it was like being cuddled by a gentle bear.

I've seen my dad described as a character, but that phrase – without a supplementary explanation – doesn't come close to doing him justice. Once seen and heard, he was seldom – if ever – forgotten. He wasn't tall – only 5 foot 9 – and he became quite stocky. He had sturdy forearms and thick thighs and a bit of a bull chest. Someone once said my dad was built 'like a muck stack', and he took that as a compliment. He had the sort of personality that filled up a room when he entered, and then emptied it again after he left. Exuberant wasn't the half of it. There was a bass-drum resonance about his voice and a throaty roar about his laugh.

No one with any gumption about them ever had to ask where he came from either. His accent belonged unmistakably to Yorkshire.

He always seemed so alive to me that at first I struggled to believe that I'd never speak to him again. Or that things wouldn't go on as before.

We lived in a village called Marton cum Grafton, which was a homely place. My dad had grown up in post-war Bradford, originally south-west of the centre and then north of it. He was a working-class boy during an era when social status was more obviously demarcated, and those on the bottom rung of it were expected to be deferential to the toffs at the top. Being 'working class' meant living in a back-to-back house, and social mobility was hard, usually solely dependent on education or the possession of a singular talent, such as sport. The only other escape was to win the football pools.

My dad was caught in a landscape that, initially at least, wasn't too dissimilar from the one that Bradford's most celebrated writer, J.B. Priestley, wrote about so nostalgically in *English Journey* during the mid-1930s. The city was the product of nineteenth-century industrialism, the sooty factory chimneys a testament to it. The place was 'determinedly Yorkshire', said Priestley. He thought it ugly and choking and claustrophobic even before some of its Victorian splendour, colliding unfortunately with the wrecking ball and the bulldozers, was replaced with the brutal architecture of the late 1950s and early 1960s. The moors, however, weren't far from my dad's front door, and that was where he went looking for space.

In Marton cum Grafton, he found his own haven. He was an outdoors man and adored the countryside. He liked the open fields, the hedgerows and the dry-stone walls that stretched towards York in the south-east and Harrogate in the south-west. Our fairly modern, mostly red-brick house had its own paddock beyond a large, wide garden. He liked to stand at the bottom of it, looking over the grassy rise and dip of the hills, which pushed themselves into the far distance of the vale. Only a scattering of pitched roofs broke the horizon. He'd observe the birds and the wildlife, calling us whenever anything interesting ran or flew into view. At night, above us was an immense arc of stars.

The seasons changed right in front of us, spread across the fields. In the spring Becky and I would hitch a ride on the back of the hay cart to nearby woods where bluebells grew thickly. The summer meant watching matches played on the village cricket pitch, which had a squat pavilion and a white-washed boundary. The autumn was rich with apples and conkers and rust-coloured leaves, crunching underfoot. And there was also the typically northern winter, the trees and shrubbery bare and the hard frosts making everything beautifully white. Strange as it may seem, my dad was incredibly fond of winter. He said he'd spent so much of his cricket career chasing the sun – abroad as well as in England – that the rain and gales and the skies as grey as pewter were refreshing for him. The more stormy the day, the more he wanted to get out into it. The wind could crack its cheeks ferociously, the rain could chuck down in torrents, but he'd still pull on a heavy coat and his Wellington boots and go for a walk. I know that what Marton cum Grafton gave us was a tranquil way of living next to the simplicity of nature. I thought of it as seemingly without end.

Delving into your childhood can be rather like walking through drifting fog. That fog is thick enough to obscure some things from you – you can't bring them back no matter how hard you try – but thin enough in parts to reveal others so vividly that they return in memory's equivalent of 4-D. So there's much I can remember about my dad then, and all of it is a comfort to me now.

I remember how much he loved our two dogs, which were Rhodesian ridgebacks. I have no idea – not even my mum does – about why he chose a breed that weighed six-and-a-half stone and can grow at a rate that makes a Shetland pony look the size of a house cat. They were not the sort of dogs you could feed on one tin of Pedigree Chum and a bowl of biscuits. They devoured the meat my dad brought back in industrial qualities from the butcher, and especially the delicacy of pig trotters, a dog's caviar. The dogs looked fearsome, but were actually gentle souls (though, I admit, our postman may not have seen them as such). One of them, called Kruger, became my dog. There's a photograph of me as a baby curled up beside him on the floor and, as I grew older, he'd sleep at the end of my bed, a guard on patrol against night-time monsters. My dad played endlessly with the dogs, who would bound towards him as soon as he came home, servants of the master of the house. He only had to look at the dogs, or give the briefest command, for them to obey him.

I remember how much he liked to tease my mum. He once brought home two huge trout with the kind of bright-black saucer eyes that seemed to follow you everywhere. He put the trout, tail first, into the freezer and packed ice around their bodies so that only the head poked out. He knew my mum would be next to open the freezer, discovering the trout staring at her, as if about to lunge at her like a freshwater *Jaws*. She shrieked the place down ... and I don't think she's looked at a trout since.

I remember how he liked to be a raconteur, a tale for every audience, and the focus of whatever was going on around him. Especially so if the talk was about cricket. He once nailed Neil Fairbrother's 'coffin' – the term cricketers use for the big rectangular case that holds most of their kit – to the dressing-room floor. Popeye, with bulging muscles and a dozen cans of spinach, couldn't have moved it afterwards. Nor did he mind telling stories against himself. Bruce French was Nottinghamshire's wicketkeeper during the years when two Championships went there. He was part of the Clive Rice and Richard Hadlee-inspired team that turned Trent Bridge into a grassy fortress, the pitch sometimes so green that it was almost indistinguishable from the outfield. On that sort of surface – and with their sort of pace and skill – Rice and Hadlee regularly found the outside edge. So scorecards almost always featured the line 'caught French' and bowled either one of them. In a career lasting 20 years, over-lapping with my dad's, he claimed over 800 first-class catches, 100 stumpings and played in 16 Tests. Before one match against Yorkshire, Frenchy sneaked a six-foot boa constrictor into the ground. The snake, belonging to his son, got draped first over the metal pegs where he got changed, slithering slowly from one to the next. The boa had a skin that was brown and yellow and green. It had a body as thick as a toddler's arm and a darting tongue that oscillated from its thin mouth. At the close of play my dad was promised that an epic surprise awaited him in the Notts dressing room. Rather too trustingly, he agreed to be blindfolded. He was led in, the walk taking place in near-silence. Frenchy took the boa in his arms and stealthily held the head of it exactly level with my dad's eyes. Then his blindfold was whipped off. My dad, so I'm told, became paler than his whites and recoiled, instantly taking two paces backwards. He thought Frenchy was about to throw the boa around his neck.

I remember how much he loved our barbecues and also being in charge of them as 'head chef'. He had a theory that meat would taste better if you lightly garnished it with beer. He had stubby cans of it, and he'd give one of them to me. He'd then pick me up, like a roll of carpet, and hold me over the grill. I'd yank off the ring pull with my index finger – my small thumb wasn't strong enough – and then send a spray of alcohol over the steaks, satisfied at the end with a dad-and-son job well done.

I remember how we used to light a fire together, scrunching up paper and fetching the wood, chopped from our own log pile. We'd watch the start of the blaze – the paper turning brown and curling, the wood slowly charring, the first whiff of the smoke and then a spark and a spit and a fabulous burst of flame.

I remember how much he liked a good pub, and the companionship he found there. It may seem odd to say this – though it became perfectly normal to me – but my dad and I spent a lot of time together in pubs.

I remember the pride he took in his vegetable patch, planting it and then prodding it as though the beans and carrots and potatoes it produced were set for a Royal Horticultural Society show.

I remember the mole traps he'd carefully lay across the lawn. I'd trail behind to check each one.

I remember sledging with him down a steep slope, climbing on to his back and clinging on, my arms around his neck. And I remember how the sledge once broke, and we fell into the deep, wet snow. As a substitute, we used an empty fertiliser bag, which whooshed along faster than the sledge had ever done.

I remember the way, if I was caught misbehaving, that one of his hands would appear as though from nowhere, and flick my ear in rebuke.

I remember the way he liked to walk around in bare feet – which is why I do that too – because, he argued, it 'toughens the soles'.

I also remember him consumed in moments of solitary thought, far away and somewhere else, the extrovert in him at rest. We had a wooden veranda on the back of the house, and sometimes – especially when it rained – he liked to put on his towelling dressing gown, brew himself a mug of tea and sit in a high-backed chair. He'd do nothing but look across the lawn in silence, listening to the steady thrum of the rain on the roof. Sometimes he'd still be there as the fields gradually disappeared into the darkness.

In recalling my dad there, I can actually see him too. He's a moving image across my mind, as surely as if I'd filmed him. The years fall away. He and I are back in Marton cum Grafton again.

THE DAY OF my dad's funeral at St Andrew's Church in Aldborough comes back to me for one reason above all others. Not because his teammates Phil Carrick, Geoff Cope, Arnie Sidebottom, Barrie Leadbeater and John Hampshire carried his coffin. Not because of the effusive tributes paid to him – particularly the 'amazing Technicolor cricketer' he'd been and the way he'd 'proceeded to the wicket like an Elizabethan man o' war' whenever Yorkshire were in a hole and he arrived to dig them out of it. Not because the vicar, so prescient and ahead of his time, said that 'perhaps' the legacy of his death would be a better understanding of the help and support sportsmen need after retiring. And not because everyone agreed that the manner of my dad's death should never be allowed to define his life; he'd been far too good as a player and far too splendid and irrepressible as a man for that to happen to him.

What I see are the crowds.

The hundreds who sat in the pews – friends, family, the dignitaries and top brass of Yorkshire beside the cricketers he'd played with and against or had coached later on. And the hundreds who waited outside, standing in sombre silence. These were faces my dad wouldn't have recognised. These were names he'd never have known. They were the people who had come, a few from a fair distance away I'm sure, simply to pay their respects to him, a last thank you for the enjoyment he'd provided, for his commitment to Yorkshire.

No doubt I had met some of them, as I gradually became aware that my dad wasn't the same as other dads; that he'd done something which set him apart. Wherever we went strangers always came up to ask him about catches he'd taken, runs he'd scored, the stellar names with whom he'd shared a pitch. Conversations would ensue about matches won and lost and the current state of Yorkshire cricket. This was fandom in the most pleasant sense, both in the enthusiasm towards him and also the respectful way in which he was approached in the first place. His hand would be shaken. His back would be slapped. He'd be offered a pint. Whoever made the offer would then plunge into a personal reminiscence, sharing the experience with the words: 'I remember when ...' My dad always added some rich memory of his own to theirs, the past replayed and wallowed in contentedly. This was long before the age of the selfie – otherwise plenty of them would have been taken – but they'd go away pleased to have met him, taking with them his words as a memento instead.

The image I have of them makes me wonder whether things could have been different. Did my dad really know how much he was loved and admired by so many people? Did he know how much those people cared and would have been rooting for him – and willing to help him get better? If he could have seen it and had it demonstrated so obviously to him – the way it was demonstrated so obviously to me at his funeral – would he have committed suicide?

It's another 'what if?' question, jostling in a long queue behind these: What if we'd arrived home half an hour earlier that night?

Would it have made a difference?

CHAPTER 2

I THINK YOU USED TO PLAY ALONGSIDE MY DAD

WINSTON CHURCHILL ONCE said: 'If you're going through hell, keep going.' It sums up our family's approach to the aftermath of my dad's death.

Becky and I passed a near-sleepless silent night, but next morning my mum got us up and made sure we washed and scrubbed ourselves, brushed our teeth and dressed for school in our plain navy and white uniforms. She insisted that we went there, though I don't remember either of us protesting much at all. It was my mum's way of bringing a touch of normality to our lives, pressing on without my dad because she knew, absolutely from the start, that we couldn't do anything else except confront, square on, the grim situation we were all now in. Already our lives had begun to change convulsively – a process that would go on until almost everything familiar to us had been rearranged or was different somehow. Knowing this, my mum came to the conclusion – and I wholeheartedly believe she was right – that we shouldn't put off doing anything today in the hope that it would somehow seem easier to do tomorrow. The fact that it wouldn't was the only certainty we had then. We couldn't think or wish away reality. We couldn't pretend it hadn't happened.

I realise now that you survive the death of someone you love simply by living, however wrong and unnatural it feels at first and however slowly it takes for your own life to find a meaningful shape again. The first task is accepting things, which is always the hardest. In sending Becky and me to school, my mum knew that the simple act of putting one foot in front of the other, walking in a straight line and holding our heads up, would be a test for us. She also knew that it was a necessary one.

Bad news travels at an alarming rate. Ours sped like a lit fuse. Shortly after dawn broke, the first reporters and photographers arrived to lean on our closed front gate, and soon an entire scrum of them were gathered there, waiting for the curtains to twitch. Becky and I had to slip out the back door and trudge over the winter fields to get to school, which was less than 150 yards down the road. In the media's eyes it seemed we had ceased to be people, who had suffered a bereavement and were in need of consolation. We became instead a story to be chased. That, I suppose, is the way of their world, but it shouldn't be. It felt like a violation.

We left my mum on her birthday – her cards unopened, her presents still wrapped – to deal with the business of death while coming to terms with her own emotions, her own trauma. She went to one of her chemotherapy sessions and discovered that the newspapers, spread across a table in the hospital waiting room, were full of headlines about my dad's suicide. The doctors, knowing of my dad's death, had wanted to cancel the session. 'No,' she insisted. 'You can't do that to me. Not now. Not after what I've just gone through.'

In the coming days there were the seemingly endless formal phone calls that had to be made to sort out finances and personal affairs. There were more calls, both incoming and outgoing, to let friends know what had happened and also how, which obliged her time and again to talk about it and answer the predictable but understandably stunned questions that came next. There were the rat-a-tat knocks on the door from newspaper reporters and well-meaning neighbours alike. There were the arrangements for the funeral.

My mum and dad had been married for almost ten years. The two of them, each recently divorced, originally met in a pub in Ossett, a market town between Wakefield and Dewsbury. My mum had just moved into a new house. When my dad asked for her telephone number, she couldn't remember it. One of her friends, who could, handed it over to him.

It was not the most auspicious of first dates. No roses. No soft music. No candlelit dinner. For some incomprehensible reason my dad decided to take my mum on a tour of some of his familiar drinking haunts in Bradford. None of them would ever have been confused with the American Bar of the Savoy Hotel. There was no sawdust on the floor, but one of the pubs had a spittoon in a corner – and it wasn't there for ornamental purposes either. The evening slipped slowly

downhill from there. My dad had a spot too much to drink, obliging my mum to take charge of his car keys and drive him home. On the way back he sang Dire Straits songs to her from the passenger seat.

A lot of women would have been washing their hair whenever he called again, offering another night out, but my mum liked his 'cheekiness' and also his 'spontaneity'. He was the sort of man who'd arrange something on the spur of the moment, seldom giving her enough time to put on a smear of lipstick and her glad rags. He was a soul, she also said, who so dearly wanted to be loved, a trait that could be traced back to being raised without his mother. She saw him as a caring and giving person, always agreeing to donate his time to causes, his match tickets to those who asked for them, his advice and expertise when needed. They moved into my mum's house until our family outgrew its small rooms. For, as well as Becky and me, my half-brother Andrew, from my dad's previous marriage, came to live with us for a while, the three of us rubbing along without any difficulty. Andrew – 14 years older than me – was someone else I could pester with a ball. He became a County Championship cricketer too, a left-hand bat and wicket-keeper at Derbyshire.

My mum is a Bradford girl; she grew up only four miles away from my dad. She planned to become a primary-school teacher. She even went through most of the training before deciding, late on, that the police force would suit her much better. If you've watched either *Life on Mars* or *Prime Suspect 1973* you'll know that some of the male officers, especially those with a considerable number of years behind them, regarded the female members of the constabulary as useful chiefly for making the tea or typing reports. You had to be twice as good and three times as resilient to avoid being marginalised or patronised – or both. My mum remembers being pushed towards domestic-abuse cases because back then these were generally seen as being 'a woman's work'. She did door-to-door enquiries when the Yorkshire Ripper was still on the loose, his identity unknown, and women were cautious about venturing out after dark, and she was on front-line duty during the miners' strike. In a career spanning 15 years, ending only after Becky was born, almost every day brought something that most of us would dread. One of her first cases was a shooting on an estate. The victim, barely alive, had shed so much blood when my mum got there that his skin was as grey as wet clay.

She was working for the traffic division – often dealing with the most grisly accidents – when she began courting my dad. Once, aware of when he was setting off for a match and the road he'd be taking to get there, she waited to surprise him, flagging down his car. My dad was chauffeuring another player, who saw only a uniformed figure coming towards them. 'Were you speeding?' he asked my dad irately, afraid that the pair of them were going to be late for the start of the match. My mum simply leaned through the driver's window, gave my dad a kiss and said: 'Have a nice day.'

Her background meant that she was used to handling other people's tragedies. She'd spent time as a juvenile liaison

officer, which demanded a particular compassion. So she'd comforted a lot of strangers who had suffered personal catastrophes; she'd been trained for that. But nothing can entirely prepare you for a catastrophe of your own – certainly not one of the magnitude she now confronted. My mum was suddenly a widow, and the responsibilities it thrust upon her – bills to pay, a job to find, two young children to care for alone – were immense. Her treatment was debilitating, sapping the strength from her body as it fought her disease. But however frail and tired she felt, and however scared she became, her first thoughts were always for Becky and me.

Ask her how she came through it all, and she'll say that her police background 'probably helped'. The trouble she saw and the situations she found herself in made her more resolute as a consequence. Then she will add, quite calmly and straightforwardly: 'And I didn't want to die. I had two young children to bring up …'

My mum spoke calmly to Becky and me about my dad's suicide. She told us that he'd been ill … that his death wasn't anyone's fault … that she'd be there for us …

At our age we got the gist without comprehending the complications, the maze of it all. There was no formal coun-selling for us, no pouring your heart out to someone who would sift through and analyse your grief as though it were a handful of sand. Our family doctor made what seemed to Becky and me casual house calls. The doctor pretended to us that he'd simply been 'passing by', but of course everything had been prearranged with my mum. Becky always made him a cup of tea. He'd then start to chat to us, working out whether we needed anything more from him.

I didn't want to go through counselling. My preference was not to speak of my dad's death. So I didn't. That was my way of coping. I had no intention of forgetting my dad or pretending he'd never existed. I loved and missed him too much for that. But I did, so badly, want to shut out the horrific circumstances of his passing. I put them somewhere in my mind where I hoped I wouldn't run into them every day. That, of course, was impossible. For sometimes thinking of him meant also thinking about why he wasn't with me – on Father's Day, and on his birthday and my own, which were only 25 days apart.

With my dad gone, I made a resolution to myself.

I would become the man of the house. Adulthood was still more than a decade away for me. My bedroom walls were covered in posters from *Gladiators*, the TV show I never missed on a Saturday teatime. But I considered it my duty nonetheless to grow up and mature overnight – and get serious about doing so. I owed it to my mum. I owed it to Becky too. I would do whatever was needed around the home. I would look after my sister, being a genuinely protective big brother to her. I would anticipate my mum's needs as much as I could, making sure I gave her as little to fret about as possible. I'd graft as hard as I could, both in the classroom and on the field. I'd make my mum proud of me. Most of all, if I had to cry, I swore to myself that I'd do it privately, where no one could see or hear me. If I found it necessary to grieve, I'd be quiet about doing so. I'd hide my hurt – just as my dad had done. And that is what I did, telling no one of my intentions. My mum remembers the two of us being in a neighbour's house very soon after my dad had died. We were standing in front of a window and staring across their garden. I looked up and said sombrely to her: 'Don't worry, Mum. We're going to be all right.'

And so we were …

THE WRETCHEDNESS OF losing a parent when you're so very young isn't confined to the sorrow alone. What's also denied to you is the chance to talk to them about their past, all the history that's wrapped up in photo albums and keep-sakes, collected and stored away. In my dad's case, I'm thinking about those simple, taken-for-granted questions. About his own boyhood and his school days, the house he lived in, the grandpa I never met and the roots of his own extended family, the places my dad saw and also wanted to see, the hopes he had.

As a child, you barely think about any of this in a construc-tive way. You might throw in an occasional 'what was it like at school during your day, Dad?', but you certainly don't think it's necessary to sit down there and then and talk about the time before you were born. The long years to come are earmarked for that.

I was lucky in one regard. At Scarborough, during the mid-1970s, my dad met the man who would become his best buddy. His name is Ted Atkinson, and it's a sign of how much he's a part of our family that Becky and I call him Uncle Ted. He spoke at my 21st birthday party and then at Becky's too. Uncle Ted and my dad were born in the same year, only months apart. He's also an only child. They shared the same sense of mischievous humour and the same generosity of spirit, soon becoming as close as brothers. The two of them could be a hundred feet apart in a crowd, but be able to detect from facial expression alone the mood the other was in and what he was thinking. I know Uncle Ted thought everything of my dad, a hero to him. I know my dad loved and trusted unequivocally Uncle Ted, someone with whom he could be himself – and also someone always prepared to tell him an unvarnished truth or two, their friendship prospering because of it.

Uncle Ted says my dad was a great bunch of blokes, which encapsulates the different sides of him. That hoary term about 'not suffering fools gladly' certainly applied to Dad. He abhorred impoliteness, for a start. If someone approached him rudely, butting into a conversation or yanking at his arm to get his attention, he'd unhesitatingly, but very quietly, tell them to 'piss off', which was reasonably mild for someone who had a master's degree in Anglo-Saxon vernacular on the field. But if he saw or heard bad behaviour off it – swearing in front of Becky and me, for example – he'd disarm the offender with an 'excuse me' and the sort of stare that could crack sheet-ice. Uncle Ted was always aware, well before it happened, when my dad was getting a bit riled this way. There were certain 'tells' in his body language. His head went up, his spine stiffened and he'd puff out his chest.

He was nevertheless much more sensitive and occasionally much more studious than any casual acquaintance – or even some of the people he played with or against – can ever have appreciated. Uncle Ted recalls my dad fretting to the extent of pacing around endlessly in circles over the plight of our kitten, which refused to come down from a tall tree after the dogs scared it. He recalls him being unable to wring the neck of a pheasant, winged during a shoot. He also recalls him refusing to budge from a spot directly in front of the television on the afternoon of Nelson Mandela's long walk to freedom, his release after 27 years in jail. He swallowed up every last second of it. 'Don't you realise,' he'd say with feeling to anyone he thought wasn't paying due attention, 'that this is a momentous occasion … and the sacrifices Mandela has made are momentous too. You *have* to watch it.'

My dad walked in the spotlight, a natural performer in the glare of it, but he would have been equally at home with anonymity. Uncle Ted makes his living predominantly as a farmer in the Yorkshire Wolds. When my dad first saw his land he pointed into the far distance and told him: 'I could peg a tent there and be content for the rest of my life.' Uncle Ted knows he wasn't kidding. My dad would gladly have opened the tent flap every morning to find fields ripe with crops or ploughed into brown ridges like strips of corduroy. If two hares were boxing in front of him, so much the better.

He also regularly hobnobbed with celebrity and aristocracy, but hated anything pompous or stuffy. He became
pally with John Paul Getty, who took him back to the lounge
of his London flat for a drink. The flat was about the size of
a South American country and full of Persian rugs and
old-master paintings. Getty rang his butler to get my dad a
drink. The butler had to walk about a hundred yards to
reach them, the sound of his well-shined shoes eventually
audible across a long corridor. He came into the room to
open a cabinet that was within arm's reach of my dad's chair.
'Blimey,' my dad said. 'I could have saved you the trouble
and poured my own.'

He still much preferred to share the company of the
old retainers of agriculture, gossiping with them to learn
the small ways and the secrets of the countryside. In the
beginning he chose to do so unobtrusively. He managed this
for a while on Uncle Ted's farm, never mentioning his own
career, until one of the men finally said to him: 'Ee lad, do
yer know yer look an awful lot like that cricketer David
Bairstow?'

I KNEW ALMOST nothing about my dad's career when he
died. I eventually picked through his past and pieced it
together from old newspaper and magazine cuttings and
copies of *Wisden* and *The Yorkshire County Cricket Club
Yearbook*. My favourite story soon became the first ever
told about him as a cricketer.

His Championship debut for Yorkshire – against Gloucestershire at Bradford in early June 1970 – seems even now like one of those *Boy's Own* stories, too fantastically neat and dramatic to be true. He was only 18, about to vote for the first time in a general election that was only a fortnight away. But there's a photograph of him, sitting a few months later in the pavilion at Worcester, in which he looks about two years younger than his age. His sleeves are rolled and he's hunched forward, self-consciously staring up at the camera as though reluctant to look straight at the lens. Apart from his ridiculously long sideburns, which were fashionable then, he seems wide-eyed and a little nervy, unsure of the etiquette of being a first-class cricketer.

Most children need convincing that their parents were once young. It doesn't seem possible. By the time I was born in 1989, my dad was the weather-beaten combatant. He had been for a long while. He carried the visible battle wounds of cricket. His nose had been broken 15 times, the bridge flattened. A cheek had been compressed. There were various other dents, gnarls and scars that cricket had inflicted on him too, the collateral damage of his honourable profession. He didn't complain but carried them proudly, each sparking a story that became benignly exaggerated with each telling, I suppose. So the photo at Worcester is a collector's item, evidence of how he'd once looked.

When the call came to play for Yorkshire, he was sitting in his school library, revising for his A levels. My dad misunderstood the message he got. At first, he thought he'd been picked for the second team. After the penny dropped, he went out to celebrate, downing two pints before summoning the courage to go back and knock on the headmaster's door. He sucked on a packet of mints, masking the smell of the beer on his breath, and told him that the match clashed with his English literature exam. Was there a possibility of bringing his exam forward? He awoke at 6 a.m., unable to eat breakfast. He sat the exam at 7 a.m., tackling the poetry of Milton and Marlowe and the novels of Graham Greene, in a draughty church hall near the school. At 9.30 a.m. he was driven to the match. At 9.45 he was standing beside the main gates, leaving tickets for his father, when Geoffrey Boycott arrived.

'Hello, David. Will you carry this?' said Boycs, handing him his bag. The two of them walked to the dressing room, where Boycs chose his spot and told my dad to put the bag down beside it. 'Thank you,' he said to him. 'You can go now.'

My dad gave him a baffled glance, unsure about whether this was a leg-pull. 'But I'm playing,' he replied. Boycs then gave him a baffled glance, equally unsure about whether he was now the butt of some small practical joke.

My dad took four catches in the first innings and another in the second. Yorkshire still lost to the team that finished bottom of the table, which says a lot about the great and sudden change in fortunes at Headingley that season.

A POTTED HISTORY lesson is necessary to explain how my dad got into the side, the challenge he faced to stay in it and why Yorkshire spent so much of the next 20 years in strife, mostly arguing among itself.

My dad's chance came because the team was in a state of flux. The 1960s had certainly swung for Yorkshire, always on an upward curve. They'd been champions six times, including a hat-trick of titles starting in 1966. They also won two Gillette Cups, then the premier one-day competition. This was the team of all the talents. Brian Close was captain for four of those Championships, and he plus Geoffrey Boycott, Fred Trueman and Ray Illingworth were the big wheels on which the side turned smoothly and ruth-lessly. There were superb players around them too. In the slips Phil Sharpe had fast hands and seemed to sense an edge before it occurred, knowing too the line and carry of it; he could have taken a catch blindfolded. Tony Nicholson was an outstanding medium-quick bowler, accurate and capable of late swing, who took more than a hundred wickets in a summer. The spinner, Don Wilson, wasn't called Mad Jack on a whim. He once batted as last man for Yorkshire at Worcester with his broken left arm in plaster from the elbow to the knuckles. He'd already hit five fours when the sixth – a straight drive over the bowler's head – won the match. There were also trusty, reliable figures, always capable of a match-winning performance: Chris Old, Richard Hutton, my dad's fellow Bradfordian Doug Padgett.

This side inspired a kind of good loathing based on envy and jealousy and a fervent desire to beat them, which was seldom fulfilled. A batsman who scored a century against Yorkshire, or a bowler who took a basketful of wickets, put themselves in contention for an England place. For some county players, facing Yorkshire was the next best thing to experiencing a Test.

But Yorkshire became complacent, assuming glory would always be theirs, and it led to some grievous mistakes. Trueman retired in 1968, and Yorkshire also let Illingworth go at the end of the same season after a contract dispute, which turned so gangrenous that he was told he could 'take any other bugger' with him when he went. The game was changing too, and, while Yorkshire remained aloof, everyone else rushed to recruit the crème de la crème of overseas stars, Garry Sobers, Clive Lloyd and Barry Richards among them. Like the Flat Earth Society, refusing to concede even the possibility of a spherical planet, Yorkshire clung to the stubborn belief that no one born outside its boundaries ought ever to wear the cap and sweater.

My dad became the stuff of Yorkshire legend, but he had to replace a wicketkeeper who was already established as such, which makes what he subsequently did even more extraordinary to me. Jimmy Binks was 19 when Yorkshire gave him his debut in 1955. He went on to miss only one match – against Oxford University – because the MCC called him into their side to face Surrey, then the champion county. Binks made 412 consecutive Championship appearances. He was part of Yorkshire's high command, consulted by captains, senior pros and frontline bowlers like a cricketing oracle. His mind was like a filing cabinet, the knowledge stored in it accrued through canny observation and those endless summers of experience. The blunt Don Mosey, his flat, gruff West Riding vowels instantly recognisable to a whole generation of *Test Match Special* listeners, put Binks's value to Yorkshire – especially during the 1960s – into crystal perspective. 'The team would rather have seen him standing there with ten broken fingers inside his gloves than anyone else with a full complement of intact digits,' said Mosey. When Binks quit in 1969, hacked off at only 33 years old with the intrusive backroom politics of the club, it opened the kind of hole that is neither easily nor quickly filled.

My dad, who as a boy had watched Binks from a bench seat at Park Avenue in Bradford, was daunted but not cowed. He found himself in a side that was still coming to terms with a new reality, which was the need to rebuild. He was being asked to take over from someone widely considered as indispensable, his like supposedly never to be seen again. When one bowler wanted a steer about a possible flaw in his action, which was the sort of information Binks volunteered without prompting, my dad told him that he'd simply 'got enough on seeing the ball' to focus on anyone else's difficulties. He was raw, untried and clinging on to the chance Yorkshire had surprisingly given him; he couldn't be expected to demonstrate in only half a season what Binks had cultivated during the previous 15. It wasn't even fair to ask. If this wasn't pressure enough, my dad immediately had to handle Yorkshire's chairman of the cricket subcommittee, Brian Sellers.

Sellers, a former Yorkshire captain both immediately pre- and post-war, had won six titles in nine years, leading some of the greatest of the great: Len Hutton and Hedley Verity, Bill Bowes and Herbert Sutcliffe, Percy Holmes and Maurice Leyland. He was once described as possessing a 'lust for victory'. Sellers was a disciplinarian, a dictatorial presence who'd been born and brought up in Edwardian England and maintained the code of conformity of the period. The anything-goes 1960s and then the still more liberal 1970s proved baffling for him. He seemed to consider Headingley as his fiefdom. He spoke in orders. Anyone who didn't march to his exact tune was in trouble. My dad described him as 'easily the most powerful and influential man in the club'. Sellers was a suit-and-tie and a short-back-and-sides man, his hair Brylcreemed with a parting straighter than a Roman road. He disliked jeans and trainers and open-necked shirts with flowery patterns.

My dad had enough going on in his life. For a start, there was the fanfare of publicity he got as a teenager, which ratcheted up expectations of him. Then there were the higher and more intense demands of the first-class game, so different from the Bradford League, where he'd played a lot of his cricket. And there was his new environment and the task of simply fitting in as a young guy around much older blokes.

Sellers could have cut him some slack. Instead he was confrontational, concerned as much about my dad's appearance as his performances, a matter someone more supportive and more sympathetic might have let slide for a week or so. One morning he told my dad to get his hair cut. The next, seeing him again, he asked why it hadn't been done. My dad made some wishy-washy excuse – based around the fact he didn't have a car – in the unrealistic expectation that Sellers would forget all about it. He didn't.

'I've made an appointment for you,' Sellers said, giving him the name of a barber's. He paid the bill in advance. He also gave the barber 'strict instructions' not to spare the shears. My dad came out looking like a ginger billiard ball.

Sellers checked up on him, growling his approval at what he saw. 'Tha' looks like a lad now,' he said. It wasn't so much what Sellers did – Yorkshire have always been strict about looking the part – but the way he did it, apparently never comprehending that his brusqueness could have been off-putting.

At the end of my dad's maiden season, Sellers got rid of Close as skipper, giving him ten minutes to decide whether he wanted to resign or be sacked. His departure created yet more instability and turmoil. The beneficiaries were Somerset, who leant on the wisdom that Yorkshire wantonly gave up and his ability to make something happen in the field when nothing seemed likely. Close became one of Ian Botham's early mentors rather than my dad's. 'Plain daft,' was how my dad saw that, regretting his missed opportunity. Close was soon making a hundred against Yorkshire rather than for them. My dad remembered it as one of his own 'worst moments'; he dropped him on 27.

EVERY ANECDOTE ABOUT Brian Close enlarges him colourfully. He was in and out of the team – he didn't play in my dad's first match – because of an injury, sustained after diving into the crease. He and Richard Hutton had gone for the sharpest of singles, and Close lunged desperately for it, bringing up a cloudy billow of dust and yanking his shoulder out of its socket. Later in the season, fit again, he chased another quick single with Hutton. Once more he was left sprawling in the dirt to make his ground. Once more his shoulder popped in the slip and slide of making it home. 'He was not very pleased,' said my dad, laconically.

Close's reputation for fearlessness and for absorbing pain was extraordinary; almost super-human, in fact. In that pre-helmet era, Close fielded as the shortest of short legs or the silliest of points, almost able to pick the batsman's pocket, and also crouched lower than a limbo dancer in his stance. In one game a shot clipped the dome of his balding head before looping over the boundary for six. In another, mid-wicket is said to have taken a catch deflected off his left shoulder blade. Afterwards, as though his bones were made of titanium, Close didn't bother to rub the welt. In a third, he got struck on the shin so hard that an enormous spread of blood soaked through his flannels, making it look as though he'd been hacked at with a machete. The Yorkshire team waited for him to wilt and fall over, but he stood his ground and gave the bowler, concerned for his health, a broadside of abuse for having not already bowled the next ball.

You'll have seen the film of Close fending off the West Indies pace attack – Michael Holding in particular – with his upper body at Old Trafford in 1976, a sacrifice that left his torso purple-black and yellow with bruising. That's the sort of man he was. Like Monty Python's Black Knight, he'd have dismissed a hacked-off limb as nothing but a scratch. I'm guessing Close saw something of himself in my dad: a lad who didn't mind a few knocks and didn't complain or make a song and dance if a small bone got broken. He just got on with things. His plain speaking endeared him to Close too – even when he was the butt of it.

My dad remembered Close being out lbw. Close thought the decision was unfair – and that the umpire was either woefully short-sighted or blind. He came back into the dressing room and went on about it endlessly. The rest of the side, wanting a peaceful life, nodded silently or murmured in agreement with him or tried to ignore the tirade, the decibel level of which increased as his indignation grew. Dad looked uncomprehendingly until Close finally stared at him and asked: 'And what does tha' think of it, young 'un?' He would not have passed the entrance exam for the diplomatic corps on this occasion. He looked at Close and said matter of factly: 'I think tha' goes on a bit.' For once, Close had no reply. It was as though someone had just poured a bucket of cold water over his head, and the sudden shock of it had robbed him of the power of speech.

He lost it again when, during a game, my dad – shedding his cap and gloves – beat him in a sprint from the stumps to the boundary to cut off a four when Close had a 30-yard start on him. He also once called him 'a prat' and somehow escaped censure. Close dismissed it as a laudable display of feistiness. Retribution of sorts came later, however. Apart from his bravery, which was taken for granted, Close was well known for four things. The first was his liking of a drink. The second was his liking for a fag. The third was his liking of a bet on the gee-gees, a copy of the *Sporting Life* his usual breakfast reading. In the morning, after checking the form, he'd draw a note out of his wallet and surreptitiously hand it to whoever was 12th man, dispatching him to the bookmakers in Headingley with the instruction about what nag in which race the cash should be placed. In the afternoon Close would send the 12th man back to discover whether the horse had won, collecting any money he was owed. The fourth – and my dad could testify to this – was his liking for driving faster than a fire engine on the way to a fire.

The fixture planners weren't always kind to cricketers. You could find yourself shunted from the top of the country to the bottom of it in the same day, a fresh game awaiting you the morning after a long trip. Yorkshire were forced to go from Scarborough to Bristol – a total of 252 miles. My dad wasn't expecting to travel with Close, who commandeered him as a passenger at the last moment. Like the perk of being able to use the 12th man as a bookie's runner, Close could choose who accompanied him to matches. Saying no wasn't an option. Not everyone wore seat belts back then, but my dad was aware of Close's reputation for slamming his foot down on the accelerator and then leaving it there. Stuffed into the boot and across the back seat of the brown Ford Capri were about two tonnes of cricket gear. My dad strapped himself in ... and then he prayed.

Close drove as if the highways and byways of North Yorkshire were as empty as the roads of Monaco for the Grand Prix. Everything whizzed by for ten untroubled minutes or so – until, with the coast well behind them, Close got further down the Driffield Road. He came to a sharp left-hand bend and then a fairly steep incline. The Capri began to tilt as Close took the bend too quickly, the weight of the cricket gear unbalancing it. Gripping the wheel with all his strength, Close fought to steady the car as a big wagon came towards them. A head-on collision was certain unless one of them managed to zag out of the path of the other. 'I honestly thought my end had come,' said my dad, who began praying again. Somehow Close managed to steer the car off the road, away from the wagon, and bump it along a grass verge. He slammed on the brakes less than a foot from a dry-stone cemetery wall. 'All I could see were grave-stones,' my dad added.

An outraged passer-by made a beeline for my dad, bizarrely choosing to scold him instead of the perpetrator. 'You should have more bloody sense than to drive like that,' he complained. Afterwards, Close turned to my dad, who was still recovering from the fright, and said to him: 'I'm glad he came to you. He might have recognised me.'

MY DAD SURVIVED Brian Close's manic driving to add another five Championship appearances to the fourteen he'd already made that summer. He also survived his first season, taking 43 catches and six stumpings, and making almost 400 runs. Yorkshire finished fourth in the table, which was smartly respectable for anyone else but unremarkable for a county so used to coming first that even second place would have been regarded as a failure.

The beginning of something can be beautiful. So it proved for my dad. His career was off and running and about to gather momentum. *Wisden* not only identified him as the 'schoolboy wicketkeeper … growing in confidence and stature' who was already 'highly regarded', but also used his photograph, a slightly blurry shot with his serge cap askew across his new short haircut, emphasising his rascally charm. He said everything had been 'so sudden' that he didn't 'think I've woken up yet'. That he failed his English exam, which had started his story, soon became irrelevant and forgotten. The following summer was calamitous for Yorkshire – it was ranked then as the worst in their history – but celebratory for him. At 19, my dad claimed more victims – 64 catches, six stumpings – than anyone else in the country, the first evidence that a new wicketkeeping era had arrived at Headingley. The rest is in the Yorkshire record books.

459 first-class matches
10 centuries, 73 fifties, a total of 13,951 runs
961 catches, 138 stumpings

He also appeared in 429 List A games, which brought 4,439 runs, 411 catches and 36 stumpings. And there were four Tests and 21 one-day internationals for England. He once claimed 11 dismissals in a match against Derbyshire, equalling the world record. In one Roses game he took nine catches, equalling the county record. In total, he got six or more victims in an innings five times. He passed 1,000 runs in a season three times. He's the only Yorkshire player to have scored more than 10,000 first-class runs and claimed more than 1,000 first-class dismissals. He won the John Player League and the Benson & Hedges Cup. He was the county's 25th captain, during a period of upheaval so wretched and severe that it made what had gone before look like a bit of playground squabbling.

My dad and the county became indivisible from one another. He was said to be the personification of Yorkshireness, a term defined as never contemplating defeat and never giving 'a toss' for anyone else's reputation.

He was some man, and he had some career, but figures and pencil marks in the scorebook tell you only what was achieved – not how. My dad's appeal lay in his pugnacious approach to the game, and the swashbuckling derring-do he demonstrated. Personality seeps through in performance, and he's a prime example of that. To realise what he was like on the field, you have to realise what he was like off it too.

He once plunged into the Caribbean Sea and split his foot on a razory piece of coral. The locals were astonished – and I mean *astonished* – that the accident hadn't taken half of his foot clean off. Blood gushed everywhere, but my dad simply bandaged up the wound and carried on with his day, as though he'd suffered nothing more serious than a nick while shaving. Also in the West Indies, he and Uncle Ted swam to a luxury boat to sample some lunchtime hospitality. They may have drunk the odd ginger beer. On the swim back, caught in a riptide, Uncle Ted found himself in difficulties. My dad, hearing him shout, remained calm, getting them both back to the beach. When Uncle Ted had a problem with an overhead power cable at his farm – the electricity company spoke gravely about health and safety and fetching a cherry-picker to remedy the fault – my dad simply said: 'I'll sort it.' He persuaded Uncle Ted to stick a wooden palette on to a forklift truck. My dad stood on it, without as much as a yellow hard hat or harness, while Uncle Ted gradually raised the thing 25 feet in the air. He fixed the damage, impervious to the danger.

I mention this because I'm sure it explains why my dad was so robust – and also how he became renowned for being as 'muck and nettles' combative as it's possible to be, an indomitable sod if you happened to need his wicket. Someone unperturbed by the sight of his own blood, dangerous sea currents and working precariously at height isn't going to be bothered by sledging, bouncers or general intimidation. What's been said of me – that I'm good in a crisis – was also said of him long before.

I know this can be said of so many players, but in a lot of respects my dad was born too early. Twenty20, with its cheek and razzmatazz and also the requirement to entertain, would have suited his gung-ho approach. He'd have liked the pulse of it – the run chase especially if it meant going up the order – and the pressure of knowing that something was expected of him. For my dad was the patron saint of lost causes – the more lost, the better. He flourished in them. He found himself in one of those circle-the-wagon stands during a 50-over day-nighter for England against Australia at Sydney in 1980. Chasing 163, England looked doomed. The six batsmen before my dad had eked out only 13 between them. When fellow Yorkshireman Graham Stevenson, making his international debut, came out to join him against Dennis Lillee and Jeff Thomson, England were on the precipice – 129 for eight. Most players in that position would have muttered a few reassuring platitudes to Stevenson about sticking in there and making an okay fist of it. 'Evening, lad,' my dad said to him as if the two of them were about to nip down to the pub for a pint. 'We can piss this.' They did. England won with seven balls to spare and both of them were unbeaten at the end, much to Australia's bewilderment. The Hill was in a daze.

At one point, with the visibility even under lights rather murky, my dad bellowed to Stevenson, 'Can thee see it?'

Stevenson bellowed back, 'I'm alreet lad,' and proceeded to bang Thomson for six.

That comeback, however spectacular, looks merely implausible beside the small task of achieving the impossible, which my dad accomplished against Derbyshire 18 months later in the Benson & Hedges Cup. He didn't so much go into bat as go into battle, coming out like a flaming arrow. You read the over-by-over breakdown of the climax of Yorkshire's innings and come away convinced there must be a misprint in the text. Surely my dad couldn't have done what he did? Yorkshire were 123 for nine in the 46th over, chasing a total of 202. That's 80 runs off 54 balls. At the other end Mark Johnson, a seam bowler, was playing in his first match. Tongue pressed firmly into cheek, my dad claimed later that he saw the outcome as a formality; there was no way Yorkshire could possibly lose. He went berserk, a flurry of hitting seldom seen before or since – even now when the climax of a Twenty20 match can constantly surprise us.

It was said of my dad that he believed 'he could intimidate the bowling simply by announcing that he was going to smack the ball over the bowler's head', and that 'often enough he kept his promise'. He did that at Derby. My dad took charge of the strike (Johnson scored only four) and dominated the bowlers with a lot of crash, bang and even more wallop. As Dickie Bird, umpiring that day, said: 'He hit it so high and so hard that I kept losing track of the ball. At one point I thought we'd lost it for ever.' He finished on 103, striking nine sixes. His last 50 was scored in under a quarter of an hour. One over from David Steele, who bowled slow left arm well enough to take over 600 Championship wickets, went for 26. Yorkshire won with eight balls to spare.

He also took a century off Leicestershire before lunch at Park Avenue – 94 minutes, 119 balls, 14 fours and 2 sixes. And his highest score – 145 – came against Middlesex and, notably, the lethal Wayne Daniel; he was memorably described as someone who 'did not know how to bowl slow' and who regularly hit a nasty length that 'tickled the ribs'. That is the polite way of saying that the 'wrong' ball from Daniel could have caved in the bone structure of your chest. My dad hit one six off Daniel that split some tiles apart on the pavilion roof.

I was too young to know all this when he died, just as I'd been too young to appreciate the titbits and threads of things that came out during those pub conversations with strangers who asked about his performances. I didn't fully realise his accomplishments, the extent of his relative fame, his efforts on Yorkshire's behalf or what it meant. And I didn't necessarily recognise any of the names he dropped naturally into his reminiscences – even though I'd already been in the company of a lot of them, especially the Yorkshire side of his vintage. My dad wasn't the sort to build a shrine to his career at home. He didn't put much of what he'd won on display. When I did see his medals and caps, his blazers with embroidered badges, the stumps and wicketkeeping gloves, they held little meaning for me. They were simply there and so taken for granted, not much more significant than the furniture. He was my dad. I loved him and he made me feel safe and wanted: nothing else mattered. Who he'd been, and also the scale of what he'd done, sunk in only later – when it was far too late to ask him about.

But a couple of years after his death, my mum took me to Headingley to watch a match there properly for the first time. I remember it was a one-dayer; Yorkshire wore a shade of flame orange, the unflattering colour of a Belisha beacon that glowed even on the murkiest of mornings. I don't remember paying too much attention to the match. I can't even tell you who Yorkshire were playing, never mind the result. I was seldom still in a seat long enough to find out. I raced about as boys do – from the rickety football stand to the open expanse of the Western Terrace and on to the Kirstall Lane end. I'd taken an autograph book with me, determined to fill as many pages of it as I could. I also had an ulterior motive. Even though I wasn't aware of everything my dad had achieved for Yorkshire, I was nonetheless as proud of him then as I am now. I wanted everyone to know it – and to know, too, that I was his son. I also wanted to collect any small piece of him that anyone else was willing to share.

So, when the chance came, I'd patiently get in line, pushing the autograph book towards the player who was next to sign. No sooner was the pen in his hand, hovering over the paper, than I'd say to him: 'I think you used to play with my dad.'

CHAPTER 3

THE PERFECT 10

NO ONE DURING my dad's day went into the County Championship to strike gold. You didn't get rich playing for Yorkshire or anyone else.

Today you have the England and Wales Cricket Board's central contracts. You can, if you're considered valuable enough, earn a few hundred thousand pounds or even a million-plus from only a few weeks in the Indian Premier League and also become a paid freelance in the other Twenty20 tournaments strategically dotted across the calendar and around the globe. The cricketers of the 1970s and 1980s had nothing like that to aim for. Their salaries, irrespective of Kerry Packer's 'revolution', didn't noticeably climb to match inflation. They made a living, but it wasn't necessarily a prosperous one and it didn't guarantee long-term financial security.

Even when he was captain of Yorkshire, my dad didn't earn more than £6,000 from a season of cricket. There were bonuses, though the county committee didn't have to pay out too many of those at Yorkshire because the team's inconsistency seldom demanded it. His main perk was a bit of mileage. There were not a glittering array of other ones. You could get a bat deal, but still have to pay, as my dad did early on in his career, for other items of kit, such as your whites or boots, and also the case in which to put them. You got the occasional item of branded 'leisurewear', such as sweaters, and the most prominent players attracted car sponsorship, the name of the company spread across the doors. It turned the driver into the much speedier equivalent of the men who once walked the city streets with enormous sandwich boards slung over their shoulders.

After the summer ended, the cricketer also had to find work to fill the blank months of winter. When the chance presented itself, my dad went on a tour or coached abroad. When it didn't, he launched himself into a variety of things, mostly relying on his personality, which meant sales and promotional work. My dad did once receive a £2,000 gift in an 85-year-old Sussex supporter's will – Geoffrey Boycott was another Yorkshire recipient – for the 'special pleasure' his 'ever-enthusiastic' wicketkeeping had given her. The benefit year, awarded on the whim of a club, was still a cricketer's rainy-day fund, the nest egg or down-payment on a pension pot from which he wouldn't start to draw for another quarter-century. The downside was that your form could suffer, becoming secondary to the effort of organising and attending events.

My dad made £56,000 from his benefit in 1982, the money gleaned from the familiar grind of dinners and matches, raffles and auctions, and also the sale of a big glossy brochure, a studio photo of him decorating the cover (he is supposedly stumping someone, the bails in mid-air and his grin a foot wider than the Cheshire Cat's). In recognition of his lengthy service and contribution, Yorkshire also awarded him a testimonial in 1990, a rarity for the county. He earned £73,000 from it. On the face of it, these sums seem high, the equivalent of a minor lottery win now, and enough back then not to worry about penny-pinching afterwards. If you sense that there's a 'but' on the way, putting those figures into perspective, you'd be right.

What my dad got was whittled away, first through his divorce and then through the gradual rebuilding of his life with my mum. We were not poor, but we certainly weren't fantastically well off either. He'd had to work hard, long hours to support us. After his death it became financially tough for us – bloody tough, actually. We had previously lived on my dad's earnings. Soon we were living predominantly on my mum's police pension. My dad's suicide nullified the insurance policy he'd taken out on himself, so money became desperately tight. If my trousers got a bit grubby, I'd brush them down and tidy them up, and say nothing about it. If my shoes pinched, I wouldn't admit it either. I'd go on wearing them to make sure my mum didn't have to buy a new pair for me. If there was a gadget or a fad, something 'must have' to guarantee playground kudos or credibility, I'd willingly go without it too. My mum would shop at discount stores to try to find the 'next best thing' for us, an item that looked a little like the one everyone else had. She had enough to do, so I was determined not to bother her with trivial things like fashion. Becky was the same. My mum took her to the opticians, not knowing how badly she needed glasses until she put them on and saw, at last, a distant street sign that before had been hazily indistinct. Becky had simply coped, believing there were 'priorities' for the family finances ahead of her own well-being.

We were always going to sell our home in Marton cum Grafton. We couldn't stay there. For one thing, we couldn't afford it. For another, too many memories crowded around us there, my dad's absence keenly felt everywhere we went. We nevertheless had to stay in the house for a further 18 months. My mum was just too physically weak to contemplate a move. She didn't get the all-clear from her cancer until 2002. The prospect of putting one place up for sale, searching for another and then packing our possessions and arranging for their removal would have been too much for her. She was so fatigued because of her treatment that her limbs could feel as heavy as stone. Even dealing with the amount of correspondence after my dad's death – the letters, the cards, the messages – had been difficult enough.

Once she was fit again, my mum wanted to move somewhere no one knew us; somewhere we could start afresh. She finally chose Dunnington, a village four miles east of York with roots so ancient that the Domesday Book records them. We initially moved into a rented cottage, thanks to the support of Colin Graves, who was then a generous patron of cricket in Yorkshire, his formal attachment to the club still to come. Finally, we moved into a house on the brow of a slight hill. At the bottom of that hill, so close that you could hit a six there, sits a manicured splendour of grass, which is the home of the cricket club. It embodies the best of the local game and the community spirit of the volunteers who run it. On match days the cricket is competitively good, the tea is brewing, the cakes and sandwiches are cut and the big hand roller on the boundary doubles as a convenient seat.

Dunnington is where we gradually put our lives back together again.

My mum saw life then as what she calls 'a series of slow escalators', carrying her from one level to another. At each level she had to stop, catch her breath and look around a while before climbing on to the next escalator. The process was then repeated, exactly as before. That's how she coped not only with my dad's death, but also with things that had to be done bit by bit as a result of it. For five years she found it difficult to celebrate her birthday. Amid her grief, still grasping for the reason behind his suicide, she also asked herself two questions. The first was: 'Did he really love me?' The second was: 'Did he think we'd be better off without him?' My mum finally put both of them aside, knowing the past would only go on interfering with our future if she didn't. 'You have to get on with things,' she'd say to us.

MY GRANDPA COLIN and my grandma Joan virtually moved in with us for six months as soon as my dad died. My grandpa fulfilled my dad's duties. No man was more important to me than him. He was a Yorkshireman without a trace of an accent, around 5 foot 11 tall. When I arrived, he'd gone bald on top, his thin grey hair growing only on the sides of his head, and he wore a pair of steel-framed spectacles. I doted on my grandpa, spending hour upon hour in his company and relying on his advice, his enthusiasm, his belief in me. I looked up to him then and I look up to him now. I always will. A good part of me *is* him.

During the war, his contribution to Hitler's downfall was becoming a member of the RAF's ground crew, an engineer working on planes such as the Lancaster, which gave him a lifelong love of historic aircraft. My grandma bought him

commemorative plates depicting them in action. My grand-parents were married for more than 60 years after meeting at a dance hall when the big bands and crooners were still at the forefront of popular music; rock 'n' roll was still wait-ing to be invented then. My grandma had worked in the corsetry section of Busby's, which was Bradford's version of Grace Brothers department store in *Are You Being Served?* My grandpa became a textile salesman, fascinated with the weft and weave of cloth and canvassing the country to sell it. I'm told he was good at the task; he even sold tartan in Scotland.

My mum so much wanted to give Becky and me the child-hood that her parents had given her. My grandpa was particularly sporty, so he took her to football matches at Park Avenue. She also played cricket with her friends on the Bolton Abbey estate, the grey stone and high window arches of the priory dominating the horizon. She ate more than one knickerbocker glory on the front at Bridlington as my grandpa, who liked sea fishing, bobbed about in a small boat in search of a catch.

I benefited from his fondness for sport too. Mother Shipton was a seer, a kind of female Nostradamus born in the fifteenth century. She supposedly foresaw the Great Fire of London, the arrival of the motor car, the ascension and the fall of kings and queens and much else besides. She didn't, as far as I'm aware, predict that her cave in North Yorkshire would become a tourist attraction just off the A1 or that a nine-hole pitch-and-putt golf course would be constructed not far from it. My grandpa taught me the game there and witnessed the first hole in one I ever got. It's one of my prized childhood memories. In our back garden he showed me how to tackle at football. Over draughts and chess, he talked to me about the strategy of sport as well. When my mum was ill, he ferried me to and from Leeds United's training ground at Thorp Arch. I belonged to their academy when, almost reviving the glory, glory era of Don Revie's 'Damned United', the club reached the semi-finals of the Champions League.

My dad wouldn't have claimed to be C.B. Fry, but he was certainly multi-talented. As well as cricket, he'd represented the county at badminton, table tennis and football, battling up front as someone you'd describe as an 'old fashioned' centre-forward. That's shorthand for being muscular and a bit rough, unafraid of getting an elbow in the face or the centre-half's studs raked surreptitiously down your calf. In the decade my dad played in you had to be as hard as the rocks on Ilkley Moor. You almost had to be guilty of manslaughter to get yourself sent off too. Not all high tackles – even those around the knees – got you booked. He made more than a dozen appearances for Bradford City at the rump end of the Football League, the former Divisions Three and Four. In one photograph of the Bradford team, taken in the early 1970s, you can tell that Brian Sellers's influence had waned at Yorkshire because my dad is crouched at the end of the front row, his hair very glam-rock and almost falling on to his shoulders; he's no longer a ginger billiard ball.

Like my dad, I began up front, before being turned into a full-back at Leeds. I was alongside two players who eventually did what I then aspired to do, which was make it into the Premier League. One of them was Fabian Delph, who not so long ago cost Manchester City £8 million. The other was Danny Rose, owner of more than a dozen England caps since going to Spurs.

Sport was my life. Each day of every week was dominated by it. I was constantly on the move and wanted nothing more than to have a go at everything. Through enormous good fortune, I ended up going to a school that enabled me to do exactly that.

MY DAD HAD been a Freemason, doing a lot of charity work, and the Masonic lodge to which he belonged came to our rescue, initiating a trust fund through the main body of the organisation. It paid for what my mum and my grandparents couldn't afford, which was private schooling for Becky and me. We went to St Peter's School in York. It changed our lives. Without our trust fund, the fees would have been well above our means. My mum had to buy part of my uniform from the school's second-hand shop.

St Peter's Latin motto is translated as 'upon ancient roads', which makes sense only when another piece of information gets added to it. The school was formed in the seventh century, making it the fourth oldest in the world. One of its first headmasters became chancellor to the Emperor

Charlemagne. Guy Fawkes was an 'old boy'. So was another of his co-conspirators in the Gunpowder Plot.

The acres of greenery there seemed to me like some sporting Eden, running on for ever.

I've always believed that you should play as many sports as possible. Each sport will develop the others. You learn different skills and disciplines that are transferable. Look at AB de Villiers, who, aged 13, joined the premier South African sporting institute Afrikaanse Hoër Seunskool in Pretoria, which found he was the athletic version of the Swiss Army knife. He could do anything. De Villiers will tell you that some of his achievements away from cricket have been mythologised. He'll simply say that he was 'decent at golf and useful at rugby and tennis'. But the fact is that he took an ingredient or two from each and dropped them into his cricket.

At St Peter's, I 'discovered' rugby, which became – and remains – a passion of mine. From it I absorbed an important lesson. When you're in an awkward scrape, you have two choices: fight or flight. I learnt it whenever an opponent, usually taller, wider and more muscular, came at me with the ball in his hands and murder in his eyes. You either tackled him or got clean out the way. The latter strategy ducked any danger of being left flat on your back, the outline of your body pressed into the turf after he'd trampled right across your chest, but it also showed that you shouldn't be on the pitch in the first place. You had to hold your ground. I'd finish a rugby match sometimes sore and exhausted, but I felt afterwards the satisfaction of being dog-weary because I'd done hard, decent work.

There were many cricketers I admired, among them Sachin Tendulkar, but the sportsman who most impressed me didn't wear white – unless he was playing for England at Twickenham. I was a fly-half, a Jonny Wilkinson acolyte and wannabe. Wilkinson could kick a ball from anywhere on the ground. He would have tackled a buffalo if it meant preventing a try. He practised almost until he bled. In everything he did and said, Wilkinson demonstrated to me not only the qualities it took to become a professional sportsman, but also what you required to remain one. I can relate to so much of what he experienced and advocated later because of it. Wilkinson only remembers feeling alive when he either held or was kicking a ball. It dominated his childhood. The game became an 'integral part of me', he said. I can identify with that. The older he got, the more competitive he became. I can identify with that too. He always had to win, he explained; he didn't want to be chewing over sorrows afterwards. I feel the same way.

His individual practice sessions, carried out alone, became all about 'grinding himself to the bone', he said. He stretched his talent further than anyone thought it would go, improving the component parts of his game. Everything about Wilkinson was focused and structured. It was all about repeat drills, which made him into a kicking machine. He'd kick for two or three hours, always believing that the next attempt at goal would improve his game. If Wilkinson kicked badly, he'd get angry with himself and stay out even longer. Even when a match had finished, everyone else in the process of leaving or already back home, he often went out on the pitch again. There were no compromises and very few days off for him. Nor was he ever afraid to do something different – hence those hands, clasped in front of him as though, like Oliver Twist, he's about to open them and ask for more.

Even when he was still learning, Wilkinson found himself driven by the fear of not fulfilling his full potential; that, he said, would have been intolerable and unforgivable. He wanted to be a real all-rounder. He wanted to be exciting to watch. He wanted to be the best, which is what he became – improving even after England won the World Cup. What impressed me was the way he thrived on responsibility, never shirking but always determined to lead ... and the way he read the game with a tactical nous only the connoisseur possesses ... and the way he was so mentally tough ... and how he conducted himself with such a quiet, unassuming dignity. Off the field he didn't grandstand or strut as 'the big I am'. On it he blamed no one for defeat. 'You create your bad days. And you create your good days,' he said, banishing excuses.

I watched his DVD – *The Perfect 10* – until my eyes hurt, using his sporting life like an instruction manual for my own. In it there's a short clip of Wilkinson on an empty pitch. He is converting a kick from fairly close range. It's early afternoon on a perfect, sunny day. He pops the ball over with a casual ease, as though this is something that comes to him as naturally as breathing. Everything is crisply sure and in perfect sync – the smooth approach, the backlift, the left leg as it cleanly follows through, sending his effort on a spin that is high and true. You look at it and know that Wilkinson could do this a million times more – and from further back – with the same result. What I'm omitting from my description is the most relevant detail of all. He's just a boy, only ten years old and still to grow and become a champion.

At St Peter's we reached the quarter-finals of the *Daily Mail* Cup, the prospect of a Twickenham final ahead. In the last seconds of the match, I was called on to take a kick that would win the tie for us. The angle was tricky – the ball hugged the touchline – and the posts seemed far off. My mum remembers some murmuring on the sidelines about the chance being too hard for me, the pressure too great. With as much Wilkinson-like poise as I could muster, I steadied myself, looking hard at the ball and hard at the target. I took a few paces back and then moved into the kick. The ball left my boot with a clean thud, reached cruising altitude and then sailed smack between the sticks. That day I felt a little like Wilkinson. We lost our semi-final, missing out on Twickenham, but for a while I contemplated a career in rugby until I realised that, physically, I probably wouldn't be able to compete in it. My uncle Ted, who is a former England under-18 manager, thought I was wrong, arguing that I could bulk myself up and soon develop the right physique.

The chances of making it in professional sport are low, but the disappointments of failure still seem particularly cruel when they occur. I've read about teenagers, especially footballers, who have been unable to handle them. A contract was their only target, their sole purpose, and their lives became fractured as soon as a coach spoke the sentence that begins with the words: 'I'm sorry, son.' I have heard that sentence. I know how it tears you up. Leeds let me go from their academy. I protested that I hadn't been given a decent enough run. I said my piece knowing it wouldn't make a difference. I think, deep down, I knew two other things too. These were:

Being cut then saved me from being cut later on.
Cricket was my game.

I know there are teenagers – again, chiefly footballers – who haven't been able to cope with the sense of loss and futility that being cast aside brings. They feel let down and used and angry. Their life, stripped of a clear purpose, has gone haywire as a consequence. I was fortunate, not only because I had cricket, but also because I had my mum, who made sure no resentment lingered. I had something else to concentrate on, she said.

At St Peter's I decided I wanted to be a professional cricketer more than anything else. I remember, during exam season, that one master saw me going to nets when almost everyone else was going to the library. 'Young Mr Bairstow off to play cricket again,' he said, 'while everyone else is in exam mode for university.' He said it quizzically, the implication that I was somehow slacking impossible to ignore. I breezed past him anyway, holding my bulging bag, and replied without hesitation: 'Cricket is my exam – and my university. And cricket is going to be my career.' I spoke the words so firmly and with such certainty, as though I'd been given a glimpse into the future and knew already what it held for me, that the master offered nothing in response.

I had startled him into a numbed silence, the way my dad had once startled Brian Close into one.

THE HEAD OF cricket at St Peter's, a post he'd held for more than 30 years, was David Kirby, a former pupil who returned to become a master, as much a part of the school as the stone used to build it. He'd played for Cambridge University in 1959, taking three centuries off the counties, scoring more than 1,000 runs and bowling some beguiling off spin. At the season's end he was picked for the Gentlemen against the Players at Scarborough in recognition of his promise. He went on to play for Leicestershire, part of the team that beat Yorkshire, then the champions, in 1961. In terms of the Championship, this was a small earthquake. Yorkshire lost by a whopping 149 runs, which was their biggest defeat since the Second World War. David Kirby was experienced and kind, good at sharpening my skills and pushing me along. He was the sort of man you instantly respected both for his knowledge and the way it was shared. I wanted to impress him.

I was fast-tracked into the school first team at 13 years old. David and fellow master Mike Johnson, also vitally important in moulding my early cricket, later said – very flatteringly – that playing me in my own age group would have turned every match into a 'farce' because I could have scored more runs than the entire opposition team. My debut was Sedbergh, a town that's one of the gateways to the Lake District. The ground there is gorgeous, a painterly view of rolling hills, a sweep of trees and the grey tower of a Saxon church. There's a chocolate-box pavilion too. It's perched on a mound, giving a grandstand view of the field.

Sedbergh, however, does tend to get a lot of rain. It had been bucketing down for days before I got there. So much so that the turf was completely sodden. The groundsman had tried to move the heavy roller from the boundary, but it sank a few inches into the outfield and couldn't be budged. He ended up cordoning the roller off with tape, which made it look like a police crime scene. Rather like the lime tree at Canterbury, the umpires decided that any shot striking it ought to be signalled as a four.

I came in at number five and the Sedbergh team looked at me the way a cat looks at a mouse. I was only about 4 foot 10 tall, which was about a foot shorter than anyone else. I was skinny too, and I suppose the pads and the bat in my hand must have appeared a little too big for me.

The pitch was a pudding, the ball coming off it so lowly

and slowly that hardly anyone so far had been able to get a shot to go much further than extra cover. If you missed a delivery, you were likely to be given out ankle before wicket. I played the first few balls defensively until the bowler decided to pitch one up, which was exactly what I wanted him to do. I saw the thing early and clearly, getting in position to smack an on drive for four. The Sedbergh side were dumbfounded, as if something possibly hallucinatory had just happened. They found it hard to believe that the small, weedy lad in front of them had sufficient strength to get the ball off the square. I got a few more off it too, making 40-odd and even pinging one against the roller.

David Kirby and Mike Johnson will tell you that I was a precocious lad. Like my dad had been, I was a 'yappy ginger fella', never afraid of voicing an opinion – or two – even in my first season. The fact that I was junior to anyone else didn't stop me from having an unquiet word with the captain if I thought the set of the field wasn't right. Or if I believed a bowler, for example, was bowling too short. Or if I spotted a flaw in an opposition batsman's technique that we could exploit. It got me into trouble once. We were doing reasonably well against a side when their supposedly most-accomplished batsman came in. There was a shower of rain and I was short enough to shelter from it beside the square-leg umpire. The game continued, and I watched the new batsman for an over or two and then said to the umpire: 'If this is the best guy they've got, I think we'll polish them off pretty soon.' No one had told me that the umpire was the batsman's father. I had to apologise to him afterwards.

I studied every aspect of the game as devoutly as a science. I know that Mike Johnson, for instance, used to smile to himself whenever I went to ask the groundsman about his preparation of the pitch, questioning him in detail about how it might play and how the recent weather had affected his work. He'd see me from a distance, a serious look on my face and my head craned right back like someone staring up at the top floor of a very tall building. 'A 13-year-old with the cricket brain of someone 33' is how he described me.

I owe so much to the chances St Peter's gave me. Financial pressure and all the red tape about compliance and health and safety means cricket in state schools has all but petered out. Kit is expensive enough. The upkeep of a row of nets, never mind a grass pitch, is prohibitive. And even those fortunate enough to have an artificial strip can't always find opponents to face over a short summer term. At St Peter's I had the benefit of first-rate coaching, first-rate practice facilities and a first-rate pitch. We also had a full fixture list.

My mum was intrinsic to my success at St Peter's. She'd be there to watch me, but wouldn't, as I sadly saw some other parents do, complain or gripe at a decision, batter the masters verbally or back them into an awkward corner with endless questions about why their son wasn't always bowling or batting up the order or fielding closer in. She once said to Mike Johnson that I'd get more attention as a wicketkeeper if I was more 'flamboyant'. The observation was so rare that he remembers it. Otherwise she brought her unequivocal support, but left behind any inclination to make a scene about it. Far too often I saw – and I certainly heard – so many parents stomp and rant on a touchline or from a boundary in the delusional belief that it was helping their son. It proved embarrassing – more so for the player, some of whom would shrivel up or lose concentration, the thread of their game gone. When this occurred, the parent became more indignant and more impossible still, and then afterwards would demand from the coach an explanation about why their boy wasn't at the top of his form. I don't remember any coach telling them to go and look in the mirror, but that's undoubtedly where the problem would be found. My mum understood, as I do now, that the frustrated parent, determined to vicariously live sporting success through their offspring, only makes life immeasurably harder for the child. It isn't just a case of being excessively pushy either. It's cloyingly needy, as though filling some void in their own past is more important than making sure the child is actually enjoying what he's doing. My mum made my life as easy as she could.

The peak of my time at St Peter's, which was like scaling a schoolboy Everest, came in 2007. In eight innings I made 654 runs, including three centuries, at an average of 218.00. My golden summer coincided with *Wisden*'s decision to establish a Young Cricketer of the Year Award, which I won. The photograph of me as the inaugural winner, which appeared on page 945 of the following season's *Almanack*, shows a piled whirl of curly hair, a blissful smile and a blazer, the white piping on the lapels as broad as a kerbstone. I look rather younger than 18.

When I went to the black-tie *Wisden* dinner in 2008, collecting an expensive leather-bound copy of the *Almanack* as my prize, the organisers let my mum and Becky come too. I was grateful for it then and even more so later on. You can't buy a ticket for this event or somehow bluff your way in on the night. You have to be asked, the grand invitation arriving on stiff white card and always crested with the woodcut of those two top-hatted gents that Eric Ravilious designed as *Wisden*'s motif back in the 1930s.

The dinner was held in London at the Inner Temple Hall, one of those imposing spaces with a high ceiling, rich wood-panelling, some heraldic shields and an assortment of oil portraits of men with whiskers and wing collars. It looked a bit like a room in Hogwarts. There was another Yorkshireman there. He'd been named as one of its five Cricketers of the Year, which in our game is akin to getting an Oscar. While I'd been getting runs for St Peter's, Ryan Sidebottom had been getting wickets for England – sixteen of them against the West Indies and another eight against India. Only a month before the *Wisden* dinner, he'd taken a hat-trick against New Zealand.

I'd come across Ryan when I was a nipper. He's over 6 foot 3 tall, and so I craned my neck upwards towards someone whom I remember looked then much the same way that he looks now – that thick curly hair like a Cavalier's from the age of Charles I. When I first met him, Ryan was still to win the first Championship of his career, which he did in 2001 as part of a Yorkshire side that included Michael Vaughan and Darren Lehmann. My mum knew him because my dad and his father Arnie played together. The names Bairstow and Sidebottom appeared on the Yorkshire score-card from 1973 until my dad's retirement in 1990. Arnie was one of my dad's best friends on the field and off it. He was an inexhaustible, loyal and reliable bowler who put Yorkshire before himself. My dad said Arnie had 'a heart the size of a mountain' and 'made my job simpler'. Spring is said to arrive only with the call of the first cuckoo. In Yorkshire, the cricket season only arrived when spectators – and a good part of the West Riding – heard my dad shout: 'Come on Arn,' urging his mate to get a wicket as he took the new ball.

I went to the *Wisden* dinner rather self-consciously, wearing a jacket that was slightly too baggy for me and a bow tie that felt uncomfortable. My mum saw Ryan and she took me over to say hello. He didn't recognise me or remember our first meeting. We didn't tell him I'd won the Young Cricketer of the Year Award, and he assumed that someone had invited us as a treat. By then he'd moved to Nottinghamshire from Headingley and seemed set to stay there. But, in 2011, he walked back into our dressing room again. And, though nearly 11 years separates us, we became so close that Ryan – we call him 'Sid' – made me godfather to his son, Darley.

No fiction writer would dare invent such a plot. It would have been too neat, too schmaltzy; and no one, including me, would ever have believed it.

CHAPTER 4

KEEP IT SIMPLE, STUPID

NO ONE SAW me cry over my dad's death for almost nine years. I hid what I felt, bottling up my emotions so tightly that almost nothing of them leaked out. And then, one August evening on holiday in Cornwall, I let go at last.

I was a month away from my 17th birthday. I was on a lads' jolly to Newquay, where we'd gone under the pretext of learning to surf, which made the week more palatable to our parents. We fought the sea, which beat us daily, but we didn't care because what had really brought us there were the bars and the nightlife. It was bliss: away from home; pretending to be an adult; celebrating the fact that exams were over; brimming with optimism about university – I'd enrolled at Leeds Met – and also hopeful of a long career in cricket to come.

One night we decided to have a barbecue on the town's Great Western beach, where the coves offer seclusion and the waves of the bay are like froth. We ran into another group, blokes of around our own age and a bit older who came from Wales. We were sitting on the sand, swapping stories, when someone began asking each of us what our dad did for a living. A few others had already replied before my turn came, all eyes swivelling towards me. I decided to keep my story as simple as possible. There'd be no mention that he'd been a cricketer; that would only have led to another dozen questions. There'd be no mention of how he died either; that could have led anywhere.

'He passed away a while ago,' I said matter-of-factly, believing the conversation would end there because decorum and decency demanded it. There was a short, slightly uncomfortable silence – nothing I hadn't experienced before – until the lad who had asked the question began staring intently back at me. His mouth slowly widened into a smirk, and then I heard a low laugh come out of him, as if death was hilarious – and that the one I'd just revealed to him was somehow especially funny. He continued laughing as I sat there, not knowing at first what to say or how to respond. Scarcely able to credit that anyone could be so insensitive, so brutally callous, I got up and marched off, wanting to get as far away as I could from him. I'd gone about 200 yards when I broke down.

My best and oldest friend is Gareth Drabble. We met as soon as I went to St Olave's, which is the preparatory school for St Peter's. He was captain of the cricket team, which is peculiar in retrospect because he prefers rugby and comes to a Test match or a one-day international only when I play in them. We seldom even talk about cricket. Gareth saw me take off and followed closely behind. I headed for a narrow pathway that ran away from the beach. For almost an hour we sat alone on a low stone wall. I shook. I raged. I cried uncontrollably ... until, finally, there was nothing left in me. Gareth had heard me deal with the odd remark or question about my dad before. He'd never seen me like this.

It was like opening a valve; and because everything came out, so everything came back in a flash to me too. My dad's death. The aftershock of his loss. Our struggle to comprehend it. Our struggle to cope. Even the fact that I'd never behaved in such a way before. There'd been sly comments in the past, the sort of snarky playground stuff that someone, who wants to bruise you without always understanding why, uses to provoke simply because he can and mainly to attract attention to himself. I'd always been able to handle it. This was different. I don't know why. Perhaps because nothing was said, but only implied, which made things worse. Or perhaps because, after so long, it was finally time for me to let go, releasing what I'd consciously suppressed. The lad on the beach proved to be the catalyst for something that would have eventually happened anyway – at some other stage and in some other spot. It was an experience I had to go through.

I confided the story to someone recently. At the end of it I said that I felt I'd embarrassed myself that day. 'No, you didn't,' he said, 'but you should have socked that guy in the mouth.'

Instead, I came home from Cornwall and put it behind me, determined to follow my dad into Yorkshire cricket, which is what he would have wanted.

IT'S HARD TO know when the love of something begins absolutely. Because of my dad, and also because cricket and cricketers were almost ever-present as I grew up, I'm sure the game was ingrained in me well before I even realised it. But I think I understood the importance of cricket – and also how important it would become in my life – in an unlikely place, which was far from our home. Bray is in Berkshire. It stands on a bend of the River Thames, and the cricket ground – home to Maidenhead and Bray – is close enough to the water to put a heaving six into it if you have the timing and the muscle.

Every year Michael Parkinson would invite my dad to play in his cricket festival. Parky has known everyone since the 1970s, when even the A-list of Hollywood's Golden Age walked down the staircase of a BBC studio and on to his talk show. I wasn't initially aware of Parky's own celebrity, so I barely recognised anyone else's. To me, he was just another of my dad's friends. The annual cricket matches he organised were a mix of showbiz and sport. Once, when I was so young that I knew nothing of the birds and the bees, I handed the *Countdown* co-presenter Carol Vorderman a box, earnestly warning her not to forget to wear it before going out to bat. She accepted my advice politely.

I recall Bray as a little paradise of blue remembered hills. I felt at home, fitting in like I'd been born there. We would go as a family, packing the car as though off on holiday, which is how it seemed to Becky and me. It was as exciting as Christmas day. The small ground, which is overlooked by a thirteenth-century church, was always dressed up for the occasion. There were white tents and striped deckchairs on the boundary, a flag and some coloured bunting around the pavilion and a brass band. It was a quintessentially English scene in high summer. Any artist, painting what was in front of his eyes, could have captured all the rich characteristics of village cricket. I remember going into the dressing rooms for the first time and sitting between heaps of kit that were scattered everywhere and breathing in the aroma of liniment and linseed oil, old wood and smoke and dust. I couldn't wait to grow up and be a part of it properly.

I'll always be grateful to Parky, who continued to invite the family to Bray even after my dad died. He didn't mind either when, aged ten, I gave him a bit of a rollicking. I'd been given my chance to play at last. I went into bat at number nine, made a decent enough score and then my partner got out. With the brashness of youth, I let Parky know in no uncertain terms that he'd made a mistake. He ought to have put me higher up the order, I said.

If Bray was the start, still remembered with a sparkling immediacy, then so much more gets folded around it in my memory. In response to charity matches that offered the chance to get together again with his pals – some retired, others still playing – my dad had a 'have bat and gloves, will travel' kind of attitude. At weekends we frequently saw glorious parts of the country, the sort of cricket grounds, similar to Bray's, that were pretty enough to illustrate calendars. My dad also occasionally coached at Ampleforth

College, which sits in a North Yorkshire valley amid woods and lakes. It looks like a stately home. The driveway to the main campus snakes so far from the main road that the journey along it seems never-ending.

However beautifully pastoral the surroundings, I knew that the game played in them required you to be as hard as handmade nails. My dad taught me that. He also spoke so proudly of Yorkshire that I always wanted to play for them and no one else, despite what I learnt, as I got older, about the divide that had opened up between them and also how much it pained him.

My future, rather than my dad's past, was more pressing for my mum, so she never allowed recent history to interfere with it. I didn't consider going anywhere else but Headingley; and I didn't consider ever leaving it when I got there – even though I had to tolerate some snide whispers that I'd been taken on and then lavishly indulged only because of who my dad had been.

MY ARRIVAL AT Yorkshire's academy proved fortuitous timing for two reasons.

The first of them was Ian Dews. He's held a lot of 'directorships' at Yorkshire: director of cricket development, director of cricket operations and director of the academy, which is the post he held when I first knew him. Ian championed me from the start. Watching me in the indoor nets, he said he immediately recognised in me 'something' of my dad, whom he hadn't personally known but had regularly seen play.

It was an enjoyable slog for me then because the demands of football at Leeds and rugby and cricket at St Peter's were never-ending. I also got into hockey, which meant I was training, playing and travelling in perpetual motion. My mum and Becky were always on the touchline or sitting beside a boundary. Kipling wrote about filling every unforgiving minute with sixty seconds' distance run. We squeezed far more out of every minute than that. My mum had a VW Touran, which guzzled petrol only because she must have done enough miles in it on my behalf to circumnavigate the globe a few dozen times. The car could have got itself from York to Leeds' training ground at Thorp Arch, so familiar did the route become. She'd also follow the Leeds team coach wherever it went on a match day, always driving because no one else on the club's books lived near enough to us for their parents to offer her a lift. The three of us dined on fast food, mostly burgers, only because there was no time for anything else. We ate on the move or we starved.

I owe a debt to my sister too. Becky and I are so much alike that we could be twins, and in childhood some strangers even assumed we were. Our personalities are similar too – though she says, probably correctly, that I'm too quick to react when something rankles with me. We had every imaginable sibling squabble: from what to watch on TV to who should sit where in the living room, and from who'd wasted the bathroom hot water to who ought to have done what household chore but hadn't.

I once accidentally hit her across the forehead with a log. It was like a scene from one of those Laurel and Hardy movies. I was carrying the log over one shoulder and turned abruptly, clocking her with it as she stole up behind me. Out came a heavy wrapping of crepe bandage. She put up with always having the smallest bedroom. She tolerated – just about – the dates I arranged secretly with her friends while, as the over-protective big brother, I baulked at her dating mine. And she never complained about my time impinging on hers. On a Saturday her friends would go shopping in York while she was watching me somewhere. Sometimes she'd have to cocoon herself in sweaters and coats to ward off the cold. At Thorp Arch she'd sit in a flat-roofed portable building doing her homework.

When I played cricket, she'd set up the picnic basket and the blanket, or she'd score, once using coloured pencils and upsetting the traditionalists who thought it sacrilegious. She always hoped there was another girl of her age there, someone she could talk to as she logged every ball. It happened rarely. One summer her holiday was the Bunbury Cricket Festival, the week-long tournament held in Newquay in Cornwall, which has become a showcase for future Test players. Becky credits me with teaching her how to catch a ball because she had no choice in the matter. In the back garden I'd shove her in goal, throw a rugby pass at her or persuade her to bowl underarm so I could practise my cover drive. She put up with all this – and more.

A few in the Yorkshire academy weren't overly enthusiastic about bringing someone in who often went away to concentrate on other sports. You were supposed to devote yourself to cricket entirely. Ian persuaded them otherwise. 'He's promising,' he said. 'Let's fit him in where and when we can.'

Ian knew that the other sports were beneficial to my cricket. Hockey improved my hand speed, built up my arms and strengthened my wrists, making them more flexible too. Rugby improved my decision-making and my reactions. Ian's opinion was: 'If you're a fly-half, standing behind the pack, you see the shape the game is taking and have to react to it quickly. You're in charge. That's going to help you at the crease too.'

He struck a deal with St Peter's. I'd always be made available for the school's crunch fixtures – Ampleforth was one of these, a match of Roses-like importance – but otherwise I played mostly for the academy. Ian made one point abundantly clear to me about this arrangement. 'When you turn out for your school, you have to be *the* star of the side,' he said. 'Don't go back there and think you can take it easy. I never want to hear that you've been lazy or complacent.'

He also curbed my tendency to be too exuberant occasionally. If someone hit two sixes before lunch, I'd want to hit two as well; and then I could get myself out attempting a third. 'Think of how many more runs you would have scored if you hadn't done that,' he'd tell me. Eventually the message sunk in.

When I was 15 years old, Ian pushed me into the under-17s, convinced that I needed the challenge. Neither that move nor his overall support of me proved universally popular. I was already familiar with some resentfully sardonic remarks, which were always made behind my back. There were two charges against me, and both of them were based around the fact that I was 'a Bairstow'.

My name had got me into Headingley.

My name guaranteed me preferential treatment there.

Sometimes Ian would even be asked: 'Are you sure he's as good as you think he is? Do you really believe he'll make it?' He was vindicated first when the under-17 side won the County Championship final.

I was part of a rare harvest of talent. It's the second reason why I count myself as fortunate to have arrived at Headingley when I did. In various teams over different summers I played alongside almost everyone that I'm playing alongside now, among them Adil Rashid, Gary Ballance, Adam Lyth and Joe Root. When I first saw him, Joe was a wisp of a thing. You'd have thought a puff of wind could have blown him away. That impression, as well as an innocent expression and those choirboy cheeks, disarmed bowlers only until the moment Joe faced a delivery, and then carnage ensued. His first appearance in the nets at Headingley was similar to Len Hutton's baptism at the club's 'winter sheds'. George Hirst, a legend, coached Hutton and said afterwards: 'There's nowt we can teach this lad.' At 12 years old, Joe sat unobtrusively watching Anthony McGrath face a session of short-pitched bowling. The ball was chucked at him hard and quick from less than half a pitch-length. When it was over, Joe asked the coach to repeat exactly the same procedure for him. At one point a bouncer clipped the grill of his helmet. He didn't care. He wasn't flustered.

I found that Joe and I were similarly obsessed. He practised constantly, smoothing out his shots by sanding away the imperfections in them. He hated not being the focus of a game. He also hated getting out. We almost always had long and profitable partnerships, but I once called him for a quick single – my fault, I think – and he didn't get home. Afterwards, far from hunky-dory about it, he complained that I'd demanded far too much of him. No one who heard the explanation (especially me) has allowed him to forget it. 'I don't have as many fast-fibres in my body as you do,' he said. Fast-fibres? Everyone within earshot was too busy laughing themselves daft to hear the rest of his protest.

EVERYONE ASSUMES THAT I'm a wicketkeeper because of my dad; that I simply got into the family business, glad to uphold the tradition of the trade he began because I so much wanted to be like him. It isn't true. I became a wicketkeeper through circumstance rather than grand design. It had nothing to do with my dad at all.

I didn't start out with any ambitions to imitate him, and I didn't feel any obligation or pressure to do so either. Early on, not wanting to slavishly follow my dad anyway, I fancied myself more as a bowling all-rounder, first of pace and then of spin. At school, I'd pull off my sweater, hand it to the umpire and reply to his question about what and how I'd be bowling with the phrase: 'Right arm over – rapid.' Soon I realised that I'd never be a successful quick bowler – I just didn't have it in me – so I turned to a bit of crafty turn and flight, giving the ball a generous tweak instead. Or at least that's how I like to remember it … I once took a six-for, the peak of my brief life as a bowler.

I was in my mid-teens before I really began to play regularly as a wicketkeeper and then to think of myself as a budding one.

With the 20/20 vision that hindsight always brings, I know my teachers at St Peter's now question whether the school should have been a bit more proactive, steering me towards the role much earlier. I can safely put their minds at rest on that score. If I'd been nagged at, or even gently 'persuaded' towards wicketkeeping, rather than coming to it gradually and in my own good time, I'd almost certainly have rebelled. I'm fairly sure that I'd have resented the lazy assumption that my bloodline should determine my future. That may sound melodramatic, but it's logical to me. Think about it. How would Stuart Broad have felt if, on the sole basis of his father scoring almost 22,000 first-class runs, the coaches at his school had forced him to bat rather than bowl? I know – since we've spoken about this – that being stereotyped because of his surname would have narked him beyond belief. In all likelihood, if I'd been given the gloves just because my dad had once worn them, I'd have turned around and given them straight back again. Maybe I wouldn't have gone behind the stumps at all.

I eventually turned myself into a batting wicketkeeper – which is always the way I've thought of things, the scoring of runs coming first – only when I reckoned it would improve my chances of getting picked for a team. It dawned on me slowly that someone had to keep wicket, so why shouldn't it be me? Ian Dews also urged me to take it seriously. 'Realistically,' he said, 'you're not going to take wickets.'

I found wicketkeeping came fairly naturally, which perhaps shouldn't have been all that surprising. I also found I liked the responsibility for the same reasons that my dad did. He kept at a much earlier age than me, undeterred after splitting a finger in his first match. His coach then insisted someone else take the gloves instead, determined to wrap him in cotton wool because of his significance as a batsman. My dad got them back through sheer stubbornness, knowing instantly where his true vocation lay.

Like him, I relished not only always being in the game, but also being at the epicentre of it – looking down the pitch, seeing the batsman and the ball with a close-up intensity. Like him, I found I preferred to see the pattern of the match unfurling right in front of me rather than peripherally from distant outposts, such as long leg or third man, where I could only half guess about whether the last delivery had swung away or zagged back. Like him, I took a lot of pleasure from setting the slip cordon and being asked my opinion about the pace of the wicket, the form and small foibles of a batsman and where a bowler might profitably bowl at him. And, also like him, I relished being the fulcrum of the fielding unit, the ball coming back to me no matter where it went, and the way you have to constantly chivvy along everyone else with a yell, a call or the loud, thudding slap of one glove into another.

The Yorkshire branch of the Noise Abatement Society probably had a fat file on my dad. I've been told how his cry of 'gedit' when a ball came off the bat or the call to 'run, run' rang for miles. You didn't need the stump microphone to hear what he was saying.

My dad never stopped talking, and he did it at full, thumping volume too. He was like a fairground barker with a megaphone attached to stereophonic speakers. The Notts all-rounder Barry Stead once came to the crease in the second innings of a game with a tuft of cotton wool conspicuously poking out of each ear. Stead told my dad that he was protecting his ear drums after the punishment inflicted on them in the first. My dad began laughing so much that his eyes grew misty with tears and he had to stop to wipe them, his vision so blurred that he couldn't see the ball.

It was said that the louder my dad shouted, the more he expected something to happen. On occasions, it did. Richard Blakey, succeeding him at Yorkshire, found himself in a quandary. He said my dad had run around 'like a maniac, barking instructions', which meant his own 'less frantic approach' in comparison brought accusations that he 'wasn't really bothered'. This made it 'hard for me to measure up to his standards', he added.

Probably through wishful thinking, people saw similarities between my dad and me where none existed. I didn't have to swot up much on technique, and I didn't swot up at all on his. I've always sworn by the acronym KISS, the principle of the US Navy. It stands for Keep It Simple, Stupid. I saw the ball; I caught the ball. There were no great dramas or histrionics about it. I didn't set out to stand out. I didn't want to flamboyantly hurl myself at a catch when good anticipation and a couple of long sideways steps would get me to it anyway. That would be making a show for the sake of it – something that simply isn't me.

My dad followed a similar template. No matter how much commotion he made, I know that he always stuck to the fundamentals. He laid them down like this: 'You have to keep thinking about the game. Keep concentrating. Keep your eye on what's going on all over the place.'

Wicketkeepers early in his era were sometimes as slight and light as jockeys, built to be nimble and nippy around the stumps on uncovered pitches. He was different, but for such a solid man there are countless accounts of his agility. He could spring upward, as though bouncing off a trampoline to take a high snick, when both the laws of gravity and geometry suggested he had no right to reach it at all. He could also stoop low, almost corkscrewing himself into the turf, whipping a hand under the ball before it licked the grass. But, generally, he wanted to see it early and get there with the least amount of fuss. 'One of the most important things is just to be comfortable,' he said. 'One of the others is not to overthink.'

His approach was partly shaped as a consequence of a rip-roaring telling off he got during a Yorkshire Second XI game shortly before his first-class debut. Impetuous and desperate to impress, he cut across first slip with a circus-like leap. He felt chuffed with himself, and expected plaudits, until the captain eyed him with a look like thunder and began bashing his ears. It was made clear that if my dad dared try that trick again, he'd be watching Yorkshire's next match – and the one after it too – instead of playing.

My dad immediately found himself likened to another Yorkshire keeper, Arthur Wood, who played predominantly between the wars. Wood was similar to my dad in physical build and background – he was from Bradford too – and also in humour. He was said sometimes to have worn 'a cap and bells', a euphemism for deliberately playing the fool when Yorkshire needed rousing or cheering up. He once shouted down the pitch at Hedley Verity, then taking a terrible caning from a batsman: 'You've got him in two minds, Hedley. He doesn't know whether to hit you for four or six.' Wood made his Test debut in an emergency, aged 40, finding himself at the Oval when Len Hutton hit his world record 364. When Wood went into bat, England were on 770 for six, and Australia were gasping. He hit 53 in an hour and a half, got out off a full toss and afterwards hurled his bat across the dressing room in playful disgust. 'Just like me to lose my head in a crisis,' he said.

Wood's zest and enthusiasm certainly sound a little like my dad's. But my dad couldn't have modelled himself on Wood any more than I could have modelled myself on my dad. He never saw Wood play, and there was scarcely any trace of him on film to study. I'd estimate that 98 per cent of my dad's performances weren't recorded either, and almost all of the 2 per cent played in front of the camera either no longer exists or can't be found. So I've barely seen him in action either.

Today we're used to watching everything from multiple angles and in super-slow motion, so nothing is missed. The camera is even capable of zooming in on a speck of dirt on the seam. When my dad played, the BBC was the primary broadcaster, but its domestic coverage, away from Tests, revolved around the John Player League and the two cup competitions. The only Championship game shown was usually the Roses match – Yorkshire TV often screened that – but those miles of film, like so much of the BBC's stock, got lost, misplaced, wiped clean or perished. What remains is buried somewhere on the dusty back shelf of an archive. There are a few short clips on YouTube: my dad standing up as well as back, taking a wickedly rising ball in front of his face, diving full length for a streaky inside edge that no one could reach or casually accepting a lobbed throw from the outfield. You frequently see nothing more than his broad back and round shoulders because the idea of putting a camera at both of ends of a ground was some way off then. There isn't nearly enough film to give you an idea of his approach or the small subtleties of his technique. You get a much better idea of his powerful stature and those surprisingly acrobatic movements from hundreds of black-and-white photographs. I reckon the photographers, knowing that if necessary he'd hurl himself after anything, however

hopeless, liked to focus on him because he was so animated and energetic. There are some striking images of my dad tumbling to engineer a run-out, stretching an arm almost loose from its socket to take a catch or sprinting determinedly after a stray ball, his lips pulled tight and his jaw grimly set. It's as though his whole future depends on cutting off a single. Captured between deliveries, he's nearly always pointing and his mouth is usually open, the instruction to do this or that or go there having just been delivered.

What made my dad a success were 'good hands'. When I was a young child, he used to plonk me on the roof of the car and I'd slide down the windscreen and across the slope of the bonnet. He'd be waiting to catch me as low as he could to the ground. There was another game, similar to that one, which my Uncle Ted says always delighted me but slightly alarmed him, even though he knew I was perfectly safe. My dad and my half-brother Andrew would throw me between them, as though I was a ball. As that song says about the daring trapeze artist, I flew through the air with the greatest of ease, apparently.

I have a pair of my dad's half-stitched wicketkeeping gloves, which are thin and flimsy compared with the much better padded modern equipment. The gloves remind me of him, but also of what being a wicketkeeper meant – and still means – physically.

At the beginning of my dad's career, the helmet hadn't been introduced to the game. At the end of it, a wicketkeeper still didn't wear one standing up to the stumps. So you were always vulnerable to a top edge in the mouth or a crack across the face. He tolerated wear-and-tear injuries: hamstring and Achilles tendon strains, a bad lower back. At the end of one season only an anaesthetic spray and a thick Heineken bar towel, wrapped tightly around his midriff, got him on to the field at all.

Of course, his hands took most punishment.

He and Uncle Ted used to greet one another with a one-armed hug and a handshake, carried out simultaneously. As my dad got older, the handshake became more difficult for him; so difficult that he almost stopped doing it, according to Uncle Ted. A lifetime of wicketkeeping left his fingers, especially on his right hand, gnarled and a little misshapen. That's what happens when, hour after hour for day after day, you take a ball that's coming at you with a lot of heat behind it. That's why Alan Knott, for example, stuck strips of Plasticine in his gloves, attempting to cushion the pounding his palms took. That's why George Duckworth bought cuts of beef from a butcher to do the same job. There was a flaw in that plan, however. In hot weather first and second slip wanted to be as far away from him as possible because the meat rotted and began to stink. But neither Knott nor Duckworth went as far as a predecessor of theirs. Herbert Strudwick was a wicketkeeping innovator for Surrey and England during the 1920s. Every night he soaked his hands in his own urine, arguing that it firmed and toughened up his flesh. It's not a theory I've ever been tempted to try.

Nowadays a wicketkeeper wears and discards two or three pairs of gloves per summer. Traditional thinking in my dad's day dictated that you used one pair of gloves for a whole season at least; for wicketkeepers bedded their gloves in, attempting to mould them to the shape of their hands like a second skin. So I know the pair that are a family heirloom contain the impression of his hands, as surely as if he'd just taken them off. When I was a boy, I could lay my own hands flat against those gloves and see how tiny they looked in comparison to his. Sometimes I'd put them on, the gloves feeling big and floppy as I tried to push my small fingers into the ends of them. It was like sliding your feet into shoes four sizes too large and expecting to walk in them. I couldn't close the gloves, the leather was too stiff and cumbersome for the little strength I had then.

But, when I had them on, it was like holding hands with him.

CHAPTER 5

THE KINGDOM BY THE SEA

WHEN YOU WALK out of the dressing room at Headingley and head down the tunnel to the pitch, you pass a banner in Yorkshire's colours. It hangs from the ceiling like a standard in a medieval court. The white rose decorates almost the bottom third of it. Sitting above are two sentences, comprising 17 words. Familiarity means that you soon learn to memorise them:

There Is a Place in Yorkshire's History Waiting for You. Are You Ready to Join the Legends?

Yorkshire has so much history, almost too much to consume, purely because of those legends. From Tom Emmett to the troublesome genius of Bobby Peel. From George Hirst to the indefatigable Wilfred Rhodes, who was still playing at the age of 53. From Major Booth, never to return from the Great War, to a score – and more – of eminent others, among them Len Hutton, Hedley Verity and Herbert Sutcliffe, and also the quartet of Trueman, Close, Illingworth and Boycott. No county has a history quite like Yorkshire's, and you're always aware of it. However much change occurs, the past is always tangible in the present – and it always will be.

The faces from yesteryear stare back at you from countless photographs, a family album like no other. Their bats, the edge as thin as a credit card compared with today's jumbo-sized blocks of wood, sit behind glass in the club's museum. Beside them are caps and sweaters, gleaming medals in boxes inlaid with silk, and cricket balls mounted on silver plinths. The leather is cracked, the seams flat and grey and ragged, but the plate inscriptions accompanying these old balls will tell you that, when shiny new, someone once took a prize haul of wickets with each of them.

Yorkshire's Championships, starting in 1893, are preserved in gold leaf at Headingley too. That list, of teams that only understood success, isn't just about boastfulness or pride. Its primary purpose, I know, is to remind every one of us about whose boot prints we constantly walk in – and what we're expected to achieve as a consequence. Even outside the dressing room, running along the labyrinth of corridors that the public doesn't see, you'll find George Macaulay or Maurice Leyland or the title winners of 1919 looking you in the eye from big display boards that detail what each of them did. It's some roll of superior wallpaper, I can tell you.

You play as a part of all this history, conscious of it trailing behind. You're another branch in an ancestral tree stretching further back even than Lord Hawke. But Yorkshire doesn't stop there. You're told, as soon as you become part of the club, that it's your responsibility to inspire the next generation the way the previous one had inspired you. You're educated from the start in the ways of Yorkshire. Even when I played for the under-11s I was taught values – the etiquette of being a Yorkshire cricketer, I suppose – and also old-school stuff. We faced other counties who looked scruffy, a bit ragtag – more like a collection of individuals than a team. We were different. You had to wear your Yorkshire blazer at lunch. You had to conduct yourself maturely. Strops, petulance and unpunctuality weren't tolerated. You had to turn out immaculately, your whites uncreased and well laundered and the rest of your kit pristine. In his teens my dad had what he called a 'great bat', a 'really whippy' thing. The ball, he said, came off it like 'nobody's business'. He used it in the Bradford League, but never in the Championship. 'It was too filthy,' he explained, knowing that Yorkshire's committee would have frowned and tut-tutted as soon as he drew it out of his bag. Appearances were so important.

It can be difficult to explain to anyone unfamiliar with Yorkshire why cricket matters so much here and why it is so integral to the county, as much a part of it as the Dales and the coastline, the market towns, the once-industrial cities and the isolated moors. Cricket has been bred in the bone for so long that Yorkshire has drawn an important sense of itself from it. Yorkshire firmly believes it is God's Own Country; and it also believes that God's own game is cricket. It isn't only enjoyed. It is studied with serious commitment.

For some – especially in the leagues – it is a way of living, every winter wished away. What's 'nobbut a game' to others is never so for them. To slightly misquote that immortal Wilfred Rhodes, cricket hasn't ever been played purely for 'fun' in Yorkshire. Winning matches is too important, the be all and end all of everything. You could even claim that the rowing and infighting which blighted the decades without a Championship were a demonstration of how much Yorkshire cared about its cricket and how much was expected of those who played it. My dad suggested it was so. Asked why passions tended to boil over so frequently at Headingley, and why everyone had always something to say about it, he replied: 'Because our heart's in it.' His certainly was – and mine is too.

I remember when Yorkshire took me on, aged 15. With my mum sitting alongside me, I waited on the hard chairs outside the club's office as one lad after another went in and then came out again. If you emerged empty handed, you'd been told that your services were sadly no longer needed. If you were clutching a large white envelope, you'd got your contract. My 'interview' lasted less than ten minutes. I came out with my envelope, feeling as though a winning lottery ticket was inside it.

I FIRST WENT on to the field in the County Championship on a cold early-August Saturday at Headingley in 2008. Almost no one noticed me.

I was nominally 13th man, meant to fetch and carry if necessary. More specifically, I was there to absorb the atmosphere and get to know some of the players a bit better, hear the banter and pick up a tip or two. Yorkshire had labelled me as someone for their future; that fact was clear and also comforting. Were it not for one thing, the game – against Surrey – would go down as a mundane, rain-hit, end-of-season tussle about relegation, which we went on to avoid … and Surrey didn't. You'd have to rake hard through your mind, or search the pages of *Wisden*, to summon a solid memory of it.

Mark Ramprakash alone made it worthwhile. He'd made 99 first-class centuries and was on the verge of becoming only the 25th batsman to reach his hundredth hundred in first-class matches, joining Grace and Hobbs, Hutton and Hammond, Richards and Bradman and the rest. Even then we knew that the achievement would be especially historic because no one would ever pass this way again; the calendar wouldn't allow it. The Championship has contracted so much, and doubtlessly will contract again soon. A batsman would need a career lasting 30 years or more – and then he'd still have only half a chance of racking up enough games to emulate what Ramprakash did.

I'd get to know and like Ramprakash later on, after he became one of England's batting coaches. But at the time he was only another of those prolific scorers whose statistics told you how classy he'd been, the sort of player you'd pay to watch and be glad to finish your career one run behind.

He'd scored over 35,000 runs, including a triple hundred. Ramprakash, then 39 years old, had gone ten innings without a fifty, but there are always moments in life that seem meant to be. He'd scored his first hundred at Headingley 19 years before for Middlesex. Now he could close the circle and complete a neat piece of symmetry. I'd expected to watch him do it from the dressing room, but first one of our team came off for treatment and then another followed him. Like the last man thrust into battle simply because no one else is available, I found myself dashing towards the square, my name announced in muffled tones over the loudspeaker. I looked around me, not entirely believing it.

Darren Gough was in charge. In terms of effort, energy and approach – the belief that a faint heart never won a jot of anything and also the absolute certainty that you could force a result simply through will and conviction – Gough could have feasibly belonged to my dad's side of the Bairstow clan. He was sure perspiration was the prerequisite for inspiration. My dad felt that way too. Gough was equally sure that you could encourage and cajole anyone into achieving anything, however far-fetched the scenario seemed at the time. My dad thought the same. He was also the sort of captain who regarded the front as the only place to be. Occupying it was a moral obligation to him; you couldn't possibly lead from anywhere else. Gough roused you to be better than you were, and he understood everything about the game except the cricketer who didn't attempt to give 210 per cent. He always did, performing as a one-man battalion. That was another aspect he and my dad had in common. I've been told a score of times – and that's a very conservative estimate – that my dad and Gough were kindred spirits, so alike that each was pretty much a mirror image of the other in temperament. My dad was there for Gough's Championship debut – at Lord's in 1989 – but made only another three Championship appearances alongside him before his career petered out. If the two of them had belonged to the same generation, the impact of a Bairstow–Gough combination on Yorkshire could conceivably have been seismic. Those barren years of the 1970s would never have happened. I wonder, though, how anyone else would have got a word in edgeways in the dressing room.

Knowing all this about Gough in advance ought to have forewarned me. I should have realised that I'd be tested. I initially supposed that he'd wave me into the outfield, where I'd be safely out of Ramprakash's line of fire. I thought I'd be posted to long leg or third man, perhaps. Gough knew, though, that I was a wicketkeeper, which to him immediately equated to 'safe hands'. And if I was good enough to be part of the squad, I was good enough not to be nursed along. 'Stand next to me in the slips,' he said. What could I do? I had enough gumption, but certainly couldn't summon the courage, to argue or tell him that I'd rather go somewhere less conspicuous. I meekly went to second slip as ordered, trying not to look petrified. I was only there for 14 balls, but I spent each of them afraid that someone – especially

Ramprakash, who was in the mid-70s by then – would get an edge. I had an image of the ball homing in on me like a missile.

The pros at Yorkshire always came to talk to those of us who one day would replace them. You helpfully found out what a bumpy ride the Championship could be before going on it yourself. Or, at least, that was the idea. That afternoon I discovered no amount of information entirely prepares you for it. You had to be in the thick of things to know what the step-up really entailed. Even being at a game was no adequate gauge. The ball was travelling around much faster than anything I'd ever come across before. I wasn't certain whether my reactions would be quick enough to take a catch – or whether I'd cling on to it if I did. Keeping my hands warm was difficult enough. The prospect of grassing a chance preyed on my mind.

Ramprakash got his century at 4.12 p.m., a forcing shot to a short ball that he sent wide of backward point. The match stopped for five minutes as he acknowledged the congratulations of his own team and the standing ovation of the crowd. I was mercifully back in the dressing room by then, applauding like everyone else. When my brief ordeal was over, I'd run off feeling more relief than elation. But I was also aware that, having survived without a scare, the next time would be easier, less daunting for me. I'd know what was coming.

I only had to wait another ten months to prove myself right.

I COULD HAVE written the newspaper stories myself, each of them understandably dominated by my dad's career and all the speculation about whether I could come close to emulating it. 'Bairstow isn't a bad name to have,' said one report. Another wondered if I'd be a 'chip off the old block'. In others there were summaries of his career, each glowing with facts and figures and recognising his contribution to Yorkshire. The pieces resembled short eulogies.

Comparisons between us were always being made. I'd got used to them, especially so when I broke into the academy at Headingley. It was easy copy to file, and I couldn't complain about that. Asked about him, I'd give an answer that may have seemed a little understated and perhaps even enigmatic to anyone who expected a long statement full of telltale emotion. 'Dad's career was Dad's career,' I'd say. 'If I can do half of what he did, I'll have a decent career myself.'

I wasn't attempting to be deliberately defensive. Or to deter follow-up questions about his death; about what that meant to me and the family; about the chance of another Yorkshire son successfully following his father into the side the way that Richard Hutton had once followed Len or that Ryan Sidebottom had later followed Arnie. I expected to be placed side by side with my dad, the match-up was unavoidable. But I didn't want anyone to think I was – or could ever be – an exact duplicate. His character was unique; he was a very singular man with a very singular approach. So my sober line about Dad's career being Dad's career was said to put all that into perspective. I meant it – and also what came next – honestly. 'I'm proud of him,' I'd say.

I was nineteen and three quarters, so I don't imagine many of Yorkshire's members had seen me play. For about a month or so before my debut – against Somerset at Headingley – there'd been a handful of publicly dropped hints about a possible call-up sooner rather than later. It was as though the club didn't want it to be a surprise to me or to anyone else. I came into the side as a batsman, finally forcing my way in on the back of an unbeaten double century against Leicestershire Second XI at Oakham when defeat had loomed.

We were three down for 44 against Leicestershire, needing 400 to win, and I was batting with Joe Root. Craig White was in charge of us. He'd been a combative all-rounder: more than 12,000 runs and almost 400 wickets. He was born in Morley, almost within sight of Headingley, but partly grew up near Melbourne in a small, former gold-mining town. On arrival, a fellow pupil told him: 'My dad thinks that the only good pom is a dead one.' White replied by punching him on the jaw. He made 30 Test appearances for England, including an emergency summons into the Ashes series of 2002–03.

He was then playing Grade cricket in Adelaide and living with his sister, who happened to be Darren Lehmann's wife. White didn't have any suitable boots, so his sister opened up her garage and told him to take a pair of Lehmann's. When White went in to bat, facing Glen McGrath – it was the first

Test in Brisbane – he found his brother-in-law at short leg. Lehmann glanced down at his feet. 'You've got my *******

boots on,' he said. He even yelled across to Shane Warne, who was fielding in the slips: 'The ******'s got my *******

boots on.' Lehmann promptly ordered McGrath to take his toes off.

There were two sequels. Lehmann wrote out an invoice and left it in the dressing room, the charge for using what he claimed were his 'favourite boots'. It went unpaid. In both the next Test and the third, White claimed Lehmann's wicket and his sister refused to talk to him afterwards, thinking he ought to have bowled half volleys that her husband could have hit for boundaries.

I mention this because it shows how steely and calm White could be. He was never going to have palpitations about our second XI run chase in the Rutland countryside. Nine coaches out of ten would have given Joe and me the instruction to anchor ourselves to the crease, presenting the bat's full face in stodgy defence for hours. Not White. He looked at the two of us and said: 'Lads, go out and entertain me.' We did, putting on 358. White was so entertained that he told Yorkshire to pick me without delay.

I stepped into a reshuffled order when Michael Vaughan was injured for the Somerset game, which began on 11 June. The date was poignant, just over a week after my dad's first appearance for Yorkshire exactly 39 years earlier.

It hadn't been, and it wouldn't become, a vintage summer for Yorkshire. Far from it. Stuck in what can be seen now as a transitional phase – Darren Gough had retired the previous season – we were already struggling in the table and barely clung on to our First Division place during the next three months, setting an unfortunate county record for the number of matches without a win. We survived, our great escape comprising chiselled-out draws.

We were regularly in the news, though seldom for favourable reasons. Vaughan, left out of the England team, made only five appearances, managed just 147 runs and retired in mid-season, deciding the sparkle had gone from his game. Matthew Hoggard, despite being our leading wicket-taker, moved to Leicestershire after the tug of war of a contractual dispute. Anthony McGrath, out of form, gave up the captaincy, handing it to Andrew Gale, who, at 26, became the youngest 'official' holder of the post since Brian Sellers almost 80 years earlier.

There's a story about a novice walking into the Yorkshire dressing room during the 1920s, the age of Holmes and Sutcliffe and Rhodes. He shuffled around outside it, peering through the half-open door because he was so apprehensive about where to get changed among the aristocracy. There was a hierarchy, a strict pecking order, within those walls. It was Sutcliffe, clearing a spot, who beckoned him in. 'Come over here, young 'un,' he said. I never had such a problem. I walked in, looked for the space no one else was occupying and plonked my kit down on it as though planting a flag; I guessed that's where I was supposed to go. I felt at home. Not many players outside Yorkshire much relish coming to

Headingley. The ground is an acquired taste and the crowd aren't slow to let an outsider know whether he's rated or not. The atmosphere can seem abrasive if you're not tuned into it. But I felt at home there too.

Somerset had a decent team, certainty superior to ours then. There was Marcus Trescothick and Justin Langer, Craig Kieswetter and Alfonso Thomas, Dale Stiff and Charl Willoughby. I fielded mostly on the outfield rather than close in. Gerard Brophy was first-choice keeper, a man with seven county seasons already behind him. In *The Cricketer's Who's Who* that year, I was described as a right-hand bat and a right-arm bowler before my wicketkeeping even got a mention. This wasn't surprising. I'd barely kept for the second XI. I'd been third-choice keeper at best at Yorkshire, behind Simon Guy, who was recovering from a cerebral abscess that had required an operation.

The match took a twist for me, turning it into one of those unlikely ripping yarns. Brophy broke his thumb. My wicket-keeping gloves and pads came out of the bag. I'd been behind the stumps only 12 times since the season began – and 90 per cent of those appearances had been for the academy. In the second innings I suddenly found myself keeping to Hoggard, someone who'd taken 248 Test wickets and was capable of swinging a delivery in front of first slip. The ball smacked into my gloves. In the 46th over Trescothick, who'd go on to score almost 2,000 runs that season, went for a drive, the ball cutting across him. He got a hard, rising outside edge. It came at me like something fired out of a cannon. I caught it – very gratefully – against my breastbone and held on for dear life, the slips able to celebrate before I could.

Looking back on his debut, my dad said that the gulf between the Championship and anything else he'd ever played in was 'mighty' because 'the ball does so much more'. It was a 'far different world' from the Bradford League, he added. He could get away with a dip in his concentration there, but would make himself 'look daft' if he did the same for Yorkshire. The first catch he took for them was critical, he maintained, because it 'settled me down' and settled everyone else down around him too. It made the others believe 'the lad', as he called himself, was rightfully in the side and had become one of them immediately. I know what he meant. I also know how he felt. I took three more catches, getting rid of Langer too.

In our first innings I made a respectable 28 before getting carried away. I tried to hit a ball over the East Stand and into the car park. It fell about 250 yards short. In our second I came in when we were 49 for three, the possibility of an ignominious innings defeat hanging over us. I batted for more than three stubborn hours, hitting seven fours in an unbeaten 82. My dad lost his first match by nine wickets. I lost mine by four, but, precisely like him, I'd made a statement, the rest of the summer now opening up promisingly in front of me.

I'd started to learn the business of being a county pro.

PERCY HOLMES LIKED to roll up first at the reception desk of the hotel wherever Yorkshire were staying and tell the clerk to: 'Book us in as Percy Holmes and his circus.' The joke, though eventually dog-eared by overuse, still had a serious edge to it. A cricket team, always on the move, is certainly a bit like a travelling circus, with all the paraphernalia and disparate personalities. You're always performing, a new audience replacing the last one soon enough. You always have to rub along with everyone.

I was as lucky as my dad had been. He made friends straight away. Doug Padgett, the opener and fellow Bradfordian, drove him around before he could afford a car of his own. And Tony Nicholson, who was fine enough to play for England but always got overlooked by the selectors, virtually adopted him. To someone still in their teens, not long out of school, anyone over 25 seems reasonably old. That means anyone over 30 seems ancient. Nicholson was 32, a former policeman in Rhodesia, and a five-time County Champion. Geoffrey Boycott described him as 'bloody good' at taking wickets. At first, my dad actually called him 'Dad' and thought Nicholson 'revelled in his paternal role'. He wasn't beyond giving him a telling-off and a clip around the ear. Nicholson soon became 'Nick', and their friendship grew out of the iron belief each had in the other's ability.

I got close to Jacques Rudolph. He was 28 years old. He'd already played in more than 30 Tests, scoring a double hundred in the first of them. It wasn't only his guarantee of 1,000 runs a season – that summer he totalled over 1,300 of them – but also the manner in which he made them that impressed and drew me towards him. He was a professional from the toes of his boots to the peak of his Yorkshire cap. The way he practised studiously. The way he shared his knowledge so unselfishly, sifting through it thoughtfully and then offering only what was most useful to me. The way he quietly pushed me on too – a nudge here, a suggestion there, a little prod to keep me straight. I didn't have 'a dad' in the dressing room, but Jacques was avuncular and I came to rely on him, knowing he'd always be prepared to talk about what I was especially interested in – batting, bowlers and the stuff it took to get into a Test team and remain there. I came to admire and respect him. He was patient with me, and never self-aggrandising.

Of course, I made mistakes. I was a whippersnapper, still maturing. Sometimes I tried to help too much. I'd rush around opening doors, making tea, sorting kit, as though justifying myself. I also got into the odd crazy scrape.

In one of them we'd gone back to Headingley to collect our cars after a game against Worcestershire at New Road in which Azeem Rafiq, who is 18 months younger than me, made his maiden hundred. Azeem had bought himself a new VW, just off the showroom forecourt. I was still semi-incredulous, I think, that I was a part of the team, and I was already daydreaming about the next match. I motored out of the car park, waving and telling everyone that I'd see them soon. I was blind to Azeem, who was stationary and directly in front of me. I bashed straight into his VW.

This wasn't the worst of it either. I lived so close to Headingley – less than half a mile as the pigeon flies – that I could almost hear the crowd clapping when a wicket fell. Yorkshire once sent out strict instructions that every player had to report in suit and tie for a club photograph. The photographer's shutter would click at 9.15 a.m. precisely.

I woke up at 9.13 a.m. Either the alarm hadn't gone off or I had slept through it. In the nanosecond my brain took to register the horror of it, I'm guessing that I must have looked like a cartoon character – eyes widening and then abruptly shooting out of their sockets on long stalks. Everything takes twice as long when you panic. I know this now. Every nerve in your body is jumping, so your coordination goes askew. You fumble for things. You can't do anything in a structured way. I began to tear around the bedroom in madcap fashion, picking up and putting down again what I didn't need and either dropping or being unable to find what I did. Imagine that scene from *Four Weddings and a Funeral* in which Hugh Grant realises he's going to be late for the first of those weddings. That was me …

I kept looking at the clock, hoping irrationally that time might have stopped or would actually start to tick backwards out of pity for me. It didn't, surprisingly. I dragged my clothes out of the wardrobe. I dragged a comb through my hair. I put my shoes on without my socks. I only half-tied my tie. I threw myself out of the front door and into the car. I got to the ground, parking skew-whiff in the first space I saw. I then ran more than 100 yards to the pitch, hurdled over the perimeter fence in a single leap and speed-walked towards the team as casually as possible, as though I could sneak up to them without anyone noticing I'd ever been absent. Not a chance of it. Everyone was waiting for me. If you tell one lie, you're forced to tell another to cover it up and then a third, which is usually wildly more extravagant than the first two.

'Car was low on oil,' I said, seizing on the first fanciful excuse that came to mind. 'I had to go to the garage.' It was unoriginal and so obviously nonsense on stilts. When the photograph was taken, I was still half-dazed in sleep, my eyes almost glued shut.

The chief prankster at Yorkshire was Anthony McGrath. You could sometimes pick a pair of socks out of your bag and discover that someone had cut the toes out of them. We suspected, but never conclusively proved, that he was the culprit – the Yorkshire Snipper. Pretending to believe my alibi, he teased the car keys away from me, offering to check the oil level on the pretext that there could be some deep-rooted problem with the engine. He knew the truth, and he also knew I'd spend the rest of the day worried sick, waiting for him to expose me as a fraud.

I did.

MY DAD'S FIRST season contained mistakes too. At Bradford, he found himself against the Surrey leg-spinner Intikhab Alam. He had never faced a 'real' leggie before, the species rare even then. You have to remember that, pitched into his debut, my dad's response against Mike Proctor was the attempt to thump one of his devilishly quick, skiddy bouncers into the middle of Malham Cove. Intikhab and his flicked wrist must have seemed to him like being given the key to the sweetie shop. He fancied his chances, he said, advancing down the wicket twice and lifting him majestically over the boundary. So far, so successful. He tried to do it a third time. Intikhab, a clever old bird, held the ball back and gave it an inch or two more air. My dad thrashed at it and was caught at long on. He'd made 26 and was 'quite pleased' with himself until he got back into the dressing room and found an apoplectic Brian Close storming towards him. In two swift movements, Close picked my dad up, pinned him against a wall and waved his finger in front of his face. 'He filled my ears with asterisks,' my dad said. 'The gist was that I had been a very stupid little boy.'

Then, during the closing weeks of the summer, my dad was so fatigued that he missed two straightforward chances, which worried him until he found Close more forgiving. He offered reassurance that it wouldn't harm his future. It was all part of his growing up, and he needed only to 'keep trying', added Close, confident that he'd build more skill into his hands.

My dad was weary because these were the early days of the John Player League, which almost doubled the amount of travelling. In one five-week period he went to Bristol, Swansea, Colchester, London, Northampton, Nottingham,

Worcester, Scarborough, Bristol again, Taunton and Manchester. It explains why his young bones were creaking a little by the end of September. To look at his packed fixture list is to appreciate how much cricket has changed. He was either playing or on the road. He was also going to grounds that no longer host first-class matches – Bradford, Hull, Harrogate and Middlesbrough among them – or no longer exist at all, such as Sheffield and Hastings, which was paved over for a shopping centre. He liked the out-grounds, once taking my Uncle Ted to Park Avenue and mourning the fact that it had ceased to be a hub of county cricket. He was so emotional as to be almost tearful. My Uncle Ted became aware of 'how much he felt the loss' of it, which had 'clearly affected him very much'.

I finished the season with six fifties, a total of 592 runs and an average of 45.53. Not bad for a rookie. I even got a not-out fifty against Lancashire in the Roses match at Old Trafford. But the innings that gave me most pleasure was also my highest: 84 not out. The personal significance behind those runs lay in the location where I scored them.

The place closest to my dad's heart, unequivocally his favourite, was Scarborough. Uncle Ted calls it 'his kingdom'. To my dad it was the epitome of the English coast, postcard perfect. He liked the look and also the feel of the resort: the bars and hotels where his friends could be found; the cafés and the fish-and-chip shops; the ruined castle on its grassy perch overlooking the harbour and both the North and South Bay; the smooth, wide beach, where countless games of cricket took place in between the sunbathers and the donkey rides, and also the way the town spread upward, from the arcades and the amusements along the front into a steep climb of roads and red-orange rooftops.

In the middle of every season he relished the change of pace he found at Scarborough – the blue band of the sea, the coastal path, the salt breeze, the seagulls wheeling and swooping. At the end of it, during the festival, the 'cricket on holiday' atmosphere, which was a kind of celebration, pulled him irresistibly towards it. Usually there was nothing particular at stake for Yorkshire there. The cup competitions were over and the title had already been decided, so the matches offered him a sense of release and freedom from the pressure of the previous five and a half months. He went to seek out a good time – on and off the field. He seldom failed to find it.

In late August and early September Scarborough was usually decorated with flags and bunting, and there'd be a band too, all of which made it rather like one of our annual jaunts to Bray. He adored the sight of North Marine Road, which was down to earth and full of Yorkshiremen who cared so much about cricket. It represented his ideal of what a ground ought to look like. There was the neatness of the brick and tile pavilion with its white-painted balcony and the spread of the 'popular' seating, the wood elephant grey. There was the terraced housing at the Trafalgar End, where someone's weekly washing could sometimes be found blowing in the wind. There was the fact that the field sat in a snug, saucer-like dip, turning it into a proper arena. He felt entirely comfortably at Scarborough.

The genial ambience of the place, the intimacy between those watching and those being watched, was unique and treasurable for my dad. For Scarborough had – and still has – something else that most other Championship grounds lack, which is a packed crowd. On sunny mornings, there'd be queues three or four deep waiting to come through the narrow turnstiles. As a player, he felt a little empty once the games were over there because it meant another summer ticked off in his life.

I first went to Scarborough as a child, taking a bat and ball so that at lunch and tea I was able like everyone else to claim my own small patch of it. There were no stern 'keep off the grass' signs there. You were encouraged to revel in the club's hospitality. Only the square was out of bounds, but you'd see a respectful gathering around the rope, the curious and the connoisseurs alike studying the scuff marks and the spider's web of small cracks on the pitch as the ground staff judiciously swept and remarked it. Around them was a mass of 'tennis-ball Test matches' as one generation, made up of fathers and grandfathers, took on the kids. You'd always be at risk of a clunk on the head, the ball from another game 25 yards away infiltrating your own, but no one minded or took offence. My dad never took part, his split with Yorkshire excluding him from Scarborough as much as Headingley; but my grandpa rolled up his sleeves, bowling when I batted.

Scarborough has always argued that letting the likes of me on to the outfield will forge an affinity not only with the club, but also with the game itself. You're more likely to go back as a spectator – and a few will go back as a player. After arriving for my first Championship match there, I let my eyes wander around the ground, stopping on those swathes of it so familiar from my boyhood, and I thought nostalgically of past times. It was another reminder of how far I'd travelled – even in a few weeks from the obscurity of the second XI.

We were playing Notts, the game beginning bizarrely. Somehow, through a quirk of wireless technology that is beyond me, the tannoy system picked up and broadcast the eulogies that were being made during a funeral service held nearby. We were in trouble when I went in – it was like my debut all over again – but I hung about for four hours, hitting ten fours and also a six. A century was in the offing until I ran out of partners, finishing 16 runs short. I wished I could have scored one for my dad.

He was capped for Yorkshire in 1973 at Chesterfield. It was a steaming hot day, but he insisted on wearing it and his new sweater throughout, the perspiration waterfalling off him. His new cap was stiff and a quarter of a size too small, making him look like *Just William*. At the end of play, he didn't stuff either the sweater or the cap among the rest of his kit, but placed them in a polythene bag as though both items were sacred. He said he kept looking at them and wondering 'whether they were really mine'.

Yorkshire knew how important Scarborough was for me. So I was awarded my county cap there in 2011. That first cap is one of the most precious things I own. The club didn't tell me beforehand that I'd be receiving it, but instead tipped off my mum, making sure she saw the presentation in front of the pavilion.

There are two moments I've always wished my dad had been alive to see. That was the first of them.

CHAPTER 6

THE POP AND FIZZ
OF CHAMPAGNE

MY MOBILE RANG, bringing up one of those 'caller unknown' alerts. I answered anyway, thinking I'd immediately push the off button when the voice at the other end launched into some nuisance spiel about insurance, double glazing or a timeshare in the sun.

It was Andy Flower.

I'd met him just a couple of times, our conversations never drifting much further than a few polite pleasantries and the odd encouraging comment about the progress I'd been making. I was only on the periphery of his orbit, so we hadn't, as yet, sat down for a meaningful one-to-one, which explains why his number wasn't in my phone – and vice-versa. He'd had to ask the ECB for it. By then Flower had been in charge of England for two years, winning both the Ashes in 2009 and the World Twenty20 competition 12 months later. Only a few weeks before calling me, Flower had taken England to number one in the world's Test rankings. And, shortly afterwards, he'd be named as coach of the year at the BBC Sports Personality of the Year awards because of that achievement.

Everyone I knew spoke well of him. He was a member of the wicketkeepers' union with 160 dismissals in 63 Tests for Zimbabwe, nearly 5,000 runs and two spells as their captain. The way he'd played for them was also the way he coached for us. From the start, he'd shown himself to be a strong, intensely focused and methodical character, who knew where he wanted to go and how he wanted to get there. He was an intelligent man who treated those under him intelligently too; he didn't talk down to anyone. Flower was also a principled character, the evidence for it shown in one unflinching and dignified act: the black armbands he and his Zimbabwean teammate Henry Olonga wore during the 2003 World Cup, a protest against the 'death of democracy' and the 'abuse of human rights' under Robert Mugabe's brutally oppressive regime. This was no token gesture, but a genuine sacrifice with risks. Opponents of Mugabe had previously been badly beaten up as a consequence of speaking their contempt for him out loud. The armbands told those who didn't know Flower something important about him. If you're willing to stand up so publicly to a dictator, then the pressures of winning a cricket match aren't likely to make you wilt.

Eventually, as one summer turned into another, I'd come to learn a lot about Flower and admire him. Like a university professor, he'd always bring his notebook into team meetings. Everything was written down, covered point-by-point and in meticulous order. There was a serious structure about his tactical approach, which had been scrupulously thought through. Flower would only confuse me when he used words that I thought he'd combed through a thesaurus to find. I'd stop him at the end of some sentences and ask for a dictionary definition.

But when he rang, there was no need for clarification. 'How are you?' he asked.

The question couldn't have been more innocuous, his way of introducing himself and allowing me an easy reply. I should have been savvier, realising straight away that Flower wouldn't have gone to the bother of tracking me down unless he had something significant to say. He couldn't be calling to just ask about the Yorkshire weather, after all.

'I'm very tired,' I told him, truthfully and without thinking.

I was still panting from a fitness test. Our season had also already been long and exhausting, an embarrassing failure for us. We'd crashed, dismally, winning only three Championship matches and finishing second to bottom. We were relegated as Lancashire took the title, a fact that only added to our misery. The occurrence of a Red Rose triumph and a White Rose disaster was too irresistible an opportunity for one entrepreneur, who produced a T-shirt with only the final table spread across it. Lancashire's name and our own were printed in capitals, the letters much bigger than anyone else's, which made the need for a witty slogan superfluous if you came from west of the Pennines. It was not only chastening, but also unexpected. The summer before we'd come close to the Championship ourselves, letting our chance go only on the last day when, against Kent at Headingley, nine of our wickets fell in 44 horrible minutes. One of them was mine. I was the last victim of a James Tredwell hat-trick. I was out for 9, which left me 82 short of my first 1,000-run season.

I'd now passed that landmark, finishing top of our averages, which was a consolation for me that didn't altogether cushion the blow of going down. After passing 50 in 18 games, I'd also gone on to score my maiden century – I even turned it into a double hundred – against Nottinghamshire at Trent Bridge. I still hadn't twigged why Flower was calling. The suddenness of it seemed implausible, so my instinctive thought about being weary came out before I realised the stupidity of saying it. Fortunately Flower chose to ignore me, getting to his point quickly.

I was in Leeds. He wanted me in Cardiff. He also wanted me there as fast as I could gather my kit, get into a car and drive the 228 miles separating us. England were facing India in the last one-day international of the series; Ben Stokes was injured, and Flower wanted me to be his replacement. My fatigue lifted. I would have walked to Wales. You've never seen a man move so fast. I was still living at my mum's, which meant a dash there, collecting clothes and bags, before the dash to Cardiff could begin. I set off around 6 p.m. and arrived at 11.30 p.m., everyone else tucked up in bed with the lights off.

That's how, during mid-September 2011, my England career began.

MY DAD MADE 21 one-day international appearances for England. One of the most memorable, he said, was the first he played in coloured clothing and under lights, both of which were still a relatively Kerry Packer-style novelty for cricket in 1979. The innovations were a vulgar gimmick for the traditionalists, but an enticement for those either entirely new to the game or who liked the idea of clocking off from work and heading to the ground. My dad initially found the lights slightly surreal, as if a football match was about to break out. The posts holding them were 300 feet high. Picking up the ball was more difficult: the bulbs of yesteryear weren't as bright as today's and weren't designed for cricket either. Throws in to the stumps from an outfield packed with shadows could be tricky to see. One of them – from Peter Willey – bashed him on the head. Like any Yorkshireman, brought up to be cautious about spending his brass, my dad went to find out how much it cost to use the lights. He whistled after being told the price: £175 per hour. The average workman back home then earned less than £2.75 an hour.

My introduction to ODIs was a day–nighter too. I was saying hello to them as Rahul Dravid was saying goodbye, the game his 344th and last appearance. We won the toss, put India in and were chasing a daunting 304 until the rain came, the target subsequently determined by Duckworth–Lewis. After some niggling, stop-start stuff, the target became 241 in 34 overs. When I came in, the floodlights burning across the ground, we were off the pace, needing 75 from 50 balls. Some thought the game was up, reckoning we'd fall far short.

Sometimes, it just clicks for you. There's no other explanation, rational or otherwise, behind what you do. I faced 21 balls in 29 minutes. I hit three sixes. The first of them – a slog-sweep – sank into the crowd at mid-wicket, a calling card to announce my arrival. The other two went out of the ground and got a soaking in the River Taff. I made an unbeaten 41 and we won with ten balls and six wickets to spare. I'll never forget Dravid's handshake, warm and sincere. Or my man-of-the-match award, so unlikely only half an hour earlier. Or the sight of my mum, overjoyed in her pavilion seat as I walked back in at the end. That the whole thing came and went in a blur, spanning less than 24 hectic hours, benefited me, I'm sure. The rush home to pack, the rush down the motorway and the rush to leave tickets at the gate crowded out the nerves and eased the pressure. No one expected much. I could throw what I liked at my innings with impunity, and so I did.

Through the unfortunate timing of his birth, my dad didn't make his Test debut until he'd played ten seasons and 183 first-class matches for Yorkshire. He found himself in the same era as two outstanding rivals and a handful of good ones. He rated the best of them, Alan Knott, as one of the 'greatest-ever wicketkeepers'. He regarded Bob Taylor, so long Knott's understudy, as a consummate performer.

Taylor played for Derbyshire. After a Sunday League game at Chesterfield, one drunken local accosted my dad as

he came into the pavilion, telling him: 'You'll never be as
******* good as Bob Taylor. You're a ******* ******,'
before kicking him twice in the back of the leg. The irony is
that my dad would never have claimed to match the purity
of Taylor's glove-work – it was as though his hands were
magnetised, drawing the ball straight into the well of his
palms – but he did consider himself to be the superior
all-rounder. Taylor's batting was so weak that he made only
one first-class hundred, finishing with an average below 17.
Taylor, ten years older, had 22 Test appearances behind him
before my dad made his first, aged 28. In late August 1979,
England finally brought him into the team for the last match
against India at the Oval. His first victim, claimed almost
immediately, was also his most prized – the scalp of Sunil
Gavaskar, caught behind.

Next to the length of his apprenticeship mine was meagre. I'd played just two and a half seasons at Yorkshire and I was only 22. But in modern sport perspective can soon slip its anchor. You're either hot or you're not, the middle ground where common sense lives usually obliterated by either hallelujahs of praise or the sort of condemnation that stings because it is so disproportionate. So it was that instantly, almost out of nowhere and based solely on one innings on a damp night, I was being tipped as a player to watch and follow, a Test cricketer of the near future, a son possessing the potential to be better than his dad. Because of Cardiff I spent the winter with the ODI squad in India and then went on the Lions' tour of Bangladesh and Sri Lanka.

I was being gently prepared for a Test series.

AT HEADINGLEY I knew the only way was up for us, primarily because the repercussions of going down still further, which would mean scrapping in mid-table or at the bottom of Division Two, were too awful to contemplate. We couldn't let that happen. Yorkshire took one of those punts that was a eureka moment disguised as a gamble. Jason Gillespie was hired to work alongside Martyn Moxon.

When Martyn first came to Yorkshire, my dad remembered someone who wore glasses with lenses as thick as double-glazing. 'With their usual sense of diplomacy,' he said, 'the team quickly decided that he looked like a frog.'

The name caught on; he's been Frog or Froggy ever since. Jason was predictably called Dizzy after the jazz trumpeter, a musician whose cheeks swelled so much on the high notes that it looked as though someone was blowing air into them with a foot-pump. Dizzy and the Frog fitted like a dovetail joint for us. Dizzy wasn't an experienced coach, but 71 Tests and more than 250 wickets for Australia meant he brought a sense of authority with him. Only five years before he'd been our overseas recruit, and the hook nose, the incongruous mullet and the size of his affable heart endeared him so much to the membership.

But I still remember how different the landscape could have looked at Yorkshire.

In 2006 the club moved for Chris Adams, asking him to restructure the whole set-up and become a kind of batsman-manager-captain-director of cricket and general man-at-the-top. It was a lot of hats to wear simultaneously.

Adams was on a high wave of success. He'd just taken Sussex to their second Championship. He'd won them the C&G Trophy final at Lord's too. He even had a Yorkshire link; his father was a Yorkie. Adams gathered us together, including those, like me, who were hopeful of eventually moving through the ranks. The meeting was held in Headingley's indoor school. I expected a cup of tea and a friendly handshake. I thought we'd then get an encouraging speech, a few rah-rah phrases that would make me and everyone else go away feeling buoyantly confident. We got a hard-line lecture instead.

From the start, Adams laid down the law. Everything was going to be different from now on, he said. What he intended was root, bud and branch reform, not a gentle nip and tuck. And what he proposed sounded to me like a dictatorship. There'd clearly be no softly, softly 'getting to know you period', and woe betide anyone who had different ideas from Adams's own. He even used a PowerPoint presentation to punch out his plans in front of us. I sensed the temperature in the room dropping towards zero the further he got into it. We all went away thinking that a kind of tornado was about to gust through Headingley, ripping up everything and scattering it goodness knows where. Change was on the way, and we had to batten down the hatches for it.

I went away demotivated and fearing the worst. Adams had already appeared at a press conference, formally confirming his appointment. He'd been forthright, confident, brisk. We didn't know that he hadn't signed his contract. Nor did we know, even as he spoke to us so bullishly, that he was having second thoughts about the job. On the way home, he performed a spectacular U-turn. He decided to stick with Sussex, insisting he'd 'underestimated just how big an undertaking' Yorkshire were asking him to make. Adams also mentioned his family's preference for the south coast, which is something so paramount that you'd think he would have established it definitively before setting off and speaking to us from the pulpit. He sounded relieved to be staying at Sussex. Most of us were more relieved that he wasn't coming to Yorkshire.

Adams was right in one respect. The club is 'a big undertaking', but the axis of Moxon, as director of cricket, and Gillespie, as coach, reinvented it. Out of the doldrums we came. No Yorkshire team had gone unbeaten through a season since 1928. We managed it, promoted as runners-up in 2012. We'd have won the title if so many of our games early and late on hadn't been weather-affected. It was as though the rain clouds were in conspiracy against us, following the team from match to match.

The core of the team was battle-hardened. There was Anthony McGrath, a Championship winner for us a decade earlier. There was Steve Patterson, who took 48 wickets. And there were Phil Jacques and Adam Lyth, each of whom made nearly 800 runs, and Gary Ballance, who made nearly 700. Twelve months before we'd been able to slide in and steal back Ryan Sidebottom after Nottinghamshire baulked over giving him the security of a long-term contract. He was only 33, which hardly made him pensionable. Our gain. Their loss.

Gillespie made one decision pivotal to me, but Gerard Brophy was so solidly dependable that I had no advance warning of it. He wanted me to be the first-choice wicketkeeper. The confidence it gave me spilled into everything I did. I got a ton against Kent at Headingley. I came within 18 runs of a double hundred against Leicestershire at Scarborough. I claimed a fifty for the Lions at Northamptonshire, which was like a mini England trial.

I'd muscled my way into becoming the logical choice for the first Test against West Indies.

At Lord's.

EVERY TEST GROUND has its own atmosphere. At Edgbaston, Old Trafford, Headingley and especially at Trent Bridge, where the floodlights of Nottingham Forest peak over the stand at the Radcliffe Road end, I've always sensed a football influence. The crowds are more boisterous, more sing-along. At the Oval, it seems as though the business community has poured en masse out of London's Square Mile to be there.

Lord's is different again. I've politely pushed my way through the crowds when either returning from a Nursery End net or after leaving the dressing room to go on to the field. I've also been inside the Long Room when it is as quiet as a church. I have gone around the gilt-framed paintings that hang on the wall – Grace and Bradman and Jardine and Lord Harris staring back at me – and I've run a hand across the top of those high-backed wooden chairs that are positioned in front of the wide windows that overlook the field. I've also looked down at the faded spike marks in the wooden floors of the pavilion, made by umpteen-thousand pairs of boots over umpteen decades of cricket, and then I've thought about all the names that have come this way before. It's as though their shadows are still there, ghosting past me. My dad, who didn't like pretension of any sort, felt suspicious of Lord's, thinking it could be rather hoity-toity. On his first visit, made as a teenager, he climbed the narrow stairs to the dressing room and went on to the balcony. He stared towards the far end and said to anyone who would listen: 'This ground's not up to much.' The slope, downhill from left to right, appalled him. He thought someone ought to level it.

I'd only played at Lord's twice before I went there for the West Indies Test: two 40-over matches, the first undistinguished, the second bringing me a century. The ground wasn't even half-full, but it felt magisterial because of the flags, the weather vane twisting in the wind, the rise of the Grandstand and the members lolling across the pavilion seats. If the Queen gave permission for a game to be staged on the lawns of Buckingham Palace, I imagine it would be like Lord's. There's always a brass band, so loud that you can hear it as you're getting changed or practising. There's always a marquee pitched somewhere too. What you get is the flavour of a garden party with a cricket match going on inside it.

In Sydney, Mike Brearley once asked my dad to go to long stop, where he got pelted with crushed beer cans and assorted rubbish and heard his parentage questioned in between every delivery. Well-hardened to the grumbling of restless, difficult-to-please crowds at Bradford and Sheffield, he found the Australians merely cantankerous in comparison. At Lord's, it's a little more genteel. I fielded in front of the Grandstand, where I could hear the pop and fizz of champagne being opened and regularly saw a cork whizzing over or past me, launched from the lower or middle tiers as though someone was using me for target practice.

We recall so much of our lives in moments, seen again like a page of snapshots, rather than a long, continuous image. So, going out to bat for the first time, I remember like this.

A breezy May day, the wind rippling in from behind the Nursery End. The clouds low. The scoreboard on 266 for four. A short, respectful nod to the departing Andrew Strauss – a century behind him, a standing ovation already underway – as we pass one another on the pavilion steps.

We'd bowled the West Indies out for 243 and had replied to the total with some conviction. We'd almost got 50 before the first wicket fell and were within a spit of 200 before the second went down. I'd been sitting on the balcony, making sure that my eyes were familiar with the dull light; though, it has to be stressed, sitting from afar and standing at the crease are markedly different. And, when you're batting at the Nursery End and looking at the rust-coloured architecture of the pavilion, it can be difficult to pick up the ball. It can vanish into one of those dark spaces shadowing the sightscreens. Or it can get lost in someone's brightly striped MCC blazer.

I was facing Kemar Roach. At 5 foot 8 he isn't the tallest quick bowler. He can nonetheless get the ball to hurry at you when it pitches short of a length. He has a fast arm, which comes down like the crack and whirl of a whip. He wore a sparkling earring in each lobe and a gold necklace that was as thick as a loop of naval rope. It swayed as he ran in towards me. The ball, only three and a half overs old, was wax-shiny, the seam stitched high and the maker's embossed stamp glowing even to the naked eye. Roach banged it in intimidatingly short. He figured, I'm sure, that I'd be nervous, a bit flustered and unsure of myself. The ball reared. I went a half-step back and almost, but not quite, shaped to deal with it by going on to my toes. Then, realising it was still climbing, I dropped my wrists and tried to wrench my chest out of the line. The delivery hit me directly on the sternum.

Welcome to Test cricket, I thought.

It was the sort of crunching blow that can knock the breath out of your body. I refused to flinch. I also refused to rub the spot where I'd been struck, thinking it would be construed as a sign of feebleness. Instead, I stood bolt upright, my expression as inscrutable as I could make it. I pretended that nothing hurt, nothing untoward had happened and nothing could cow me or disturb my composure. The ball dropped harmlessly with a soft thud towards the slips, where Darren Sammy, the West Indies captain, narrowed his gaze, cast it towards me and said in his richly deep Saint Lucian accent, deliberately loud enough for me to hear: 'Oh boys, we got a brave one here. A real brave one. You hit him and he don't go down.'

I comforted myself with the thought that it could have been worse. Even a batsman as classically fine as Jimmy Cook – more than 21,000 first-class runs – got a first-ball duck in his Test debut for South Africa. I was still there, another two deliveries of Roach's over to come. However much the wound stung, the outline of the seam possibly tattooed on to my chest, I wouldn't be in the record books as someone who got a first-baller at Lord's, which is the kind of fact that would have followed me for ever. After that, I steadied myself and managed to make some shots, including a handsome drive. I got in – but then I got out. Roach claimed his revenge, trapping me lbw for 16, the ball jagging down the slope that my dad disliked so much.

We won that Test by five wickets, and the second at Trent Bridge even more overwhelmingly, steamrollering them by nine wickets. The third, at Edgbaston, ended as a draw, a fierce barrage of rain settling over Birmingham and refusing to move. The first two days were washed out, making what was left largely redundant, a result impossible. My first Test series was over, and I'd batted only three more times (one of those was a nought not out). I'd patched together 38 runs, inspiring no poetry.

Now, when I look back on it, I think I probably wasn't ready for England at that stage. But I also know that if I hadn't played then – if Andrew Strauss and Andy Flower hadn't backed me – I wouldn't have been as successful subsequently. If not then, when? If not against the West Indies, then whom?

I learnt painfully – as that ball from Roach flew towards me – that the difference between the County Championship and a Test match is half a second; sometimes even less than that. Not even a full tick-tock of the clock. Doesn't seem much, does it? Everything, though, is speeded up in a Test – especially the ball when it's coming at you – in comparison with the Championship. For Yorkshire, I was used to getting two balls an over to score off. For England, I might not get one. Your temperament as much as your talent is on trial. A coach can talk to you about all this for hours, but you have to experience five minutes first-hand to understand it properly. I learnt that at Lord's, which meant I benefited from it later on.

I was the 87th player to make his Test debut for England there, which is a nice statistic but not as significant as another. I was the 13th son to follow his dad into the England team, a sequence that began in the mid-1930s when David Townsend, an opener and the last man to be capped without playing for a first-class county, emulated what his father Charlie – an all-rounder who bowled slow right-arm and batted left-handed for Gloucestershire – did in 1899. Among those who achieved the feat after them are some names you'll find in a hall of fame, such as the Tates, Fred and Maurice; the Joe Hardstaffs, senior and junior; the Manns, Frank and George; the Huttons, Len and Richard; and, much more recently, the Broads, Chris and Stuart. There was only one difference between me and everyone else who had gone before. I was the only son whose dad wasn't there to see him play.

My dad said he always remembered a John Player League game at Hull against Hampshire. Geoffrey Boycott was out lbw to a shooter, a horror of a delivery skimming so low that the ball trimmed the grass of a shorn pitch. As a novice, my dad couldn't understand why, as soon as the umpire's finger passed sentence, everyone around him began dashing out of the dressing room. It was as though someone had just shouted 'Fire!' 'They fled through the door,' he said. Boycs, fuming at such rotten luck, arrived in a rage of industrial language, which began after a bit of bat tossing. My dad sat as impassively as possible through the worst of it. This seemed to impress Boycs, who gained a respect for him. The two of them stayed pals even through the turbulent years at Yorkshire.

Boycs and his wife Rachael have been so helpful to my mum. They let her use their home in South Africa and we went as a family later too, spending a Christmas there. Boycs has seen me grow up, once even coming to watch me play football, but has never interfered. I've known nonetheless that he and Rachael are always willing to support the three of us, however and wherever possible.

So it was appropriate that Boycs should present me with my England cap, shaking hands and telling me in that unmis-takable voice, which most at one time or another have tried to imitate: 'Your dad would have been so proud of you today.'

I knew it was true, but I so wanted my dad to have been there, so I could have heard him say it instead.

My Test debut at Lord's was the second thing I wish he'd seen.

CHAPTER 7

THE SMALLEST ROOM AT LORD'S

I HAD NEVER been to an Ashes Test before I played in one; everything I knew about the colour and the atmosphere of the series had been gleaned from television.

Like everyone else, caught in the wild fever of it, the 2005 series gripped me wholly from start to tumultuous finish, making the others I'd seen before it seem palely inconsequential. In those seven crazy weeks it became impossible to look away. You were too afraid of missing something. You searched out a TV or radio and you turned every day to the newspaper back pages. It was suddenly fashionable to be into cricket. Even people who previously had been only loosely interested in the game became utterly absorbed in it, as though the series was another soap opera. Wherever you went someone was talking, like an expert, about tactics or the personalities of Andrew Flintoff or Kevin Pietersen, Shane Warne or Ricky Ponting.

The images of those Tests have since been played and replayed so often that constant repetition has affixed them to the mind. We can always summon back the most memorable of them: that Steve Harmison bouncer at Lord's, which gashed Ponting's cheek after pounding him on the side of the helmet, the blood that came from the cut proving that the Australians were really human like the rest of us ... Flintoff draping his left arm over Brett Lee's right shoulder in an act of Corinthian compassion at Edgbaston, a scene worthy of some grand oil painting as well as the photograph that captured it ... the swarm and heave of the crowd as it queued outside Old Trafford, the compulsion to *be there* and be a part of the match irresistible ... the dive, the rise of dust and then the splayed stumps at Trent Bridge after Gary Pratt's run-out of Ponting ... and finally the pandemonium of the Oval, where there was enough confetti for a thousand and one weddings and enough champagne for a thousand and one more. A series like that, with the bonus of a cliff-hanging last day of suspense, comes around rarely, like some grand comet. You count yourself, as I did, grateful and privileged to have witnessed it.

I'd grown up in the age of Baggy Green dominance. I wasn't a glint in anyone's eye when, in 1986–87, the team that supposedly couldn't bat, bowl or field – even though Ian Botham was in it – brought the Ashes back from Australia under Mike Gatting. In the year I was born, we lost them again. My generation grew up so familiar with England not owning the urn that it seemed as though there would be no end to the sequence of disappointments. The Aussies looked invulnerable; they came and then conquered or we'd go down there and get our butts kicked. As spectators we became fatalistic about it, glumly taking defeat almost for granted and consoling ourselves with thoughts of 'the next time'. So in 2005 we rooted from our hearts to our boots for what we eventually got, but we never believed it would happen until it actually did. We had our stiff upper-lip ready again – just in case victory slid inexplicably away from us at the very moment we went to grasp it.

That sweetest of summers also answered the question of sport's place in life's great scheme. You'll always find hardened naysayers who think getting carried away about winning on a field is frivolous when the world has more important issues to concern it. But what 2005 did was underscore sport's capacity to have a dazzling effect on morale. This was more than simply 'a sporting win'. This was a catharsis too. We felt better about ourselves because of it.

I was a fortnight away from my 16th birthday when that series ended. My hero worship throughout it belonged to Ian Bell – though I don't think I've ever made that abundantly clear to him. He was the baby of the England team. He was only 23 and had played in just three Tests before being pitched into it. He didn't get a substantial amount of runs against the Australians. Apart from making fifties in both innings at Old Trafford, the limelight didn't track him the way it did Flintoff or Pietersen. But sometimes just the fluidity of a single shot – a cover drive or something wristy or powerfully straight – was so well-timed, so beautifully exquisite in its execution that it amazed me. He didn't go in for flashy, show-off strokes, but everything was still stylish.

He was neat and gracefully compact, his movement gorgeous to watch. I didn't want to miss a ball when he came in, thinking I could learn something. I would have paid at the gate to study him alone. Even his walk to the wicket had an authority about it.

He had a Slazenger bat. I had a Slazenger bat too, and in the nets at St Peter's School I tried to copy him – the lovely arc of his pick-up, the lovelier follow-through. He'd sometimes hold the final position of the shot, as though posing for a sculptor who was about to start chipping away at some vast block of stone. I know there are spectators old enough to talk with first-hand knowledge about the greats, such as Wally Hammond and Tom Graveney, both of whom had a signature flourish to their shot-making, especially through the covers. But I can't believe either of them – or anyone else – had more aesthetic appeal than Bell. Not for me anyhow.

I watched him with awe and I wanted to be like him. I also wanted to play against Australia, but it was not the sort of private thought you made too public because it sounded fanciful – even more crazy than telling everyone you planned to fly to the moon simply by flapping your arms. But less than eight years later, on an overcast early afternoon, I came down the shallow drop of stone steps that lead out of the wooden pavilion at Trent Bridge. It was my first Ashes Test. We were batting on a pitch that was the colour of parched wheat. We were in a bit of trouble: 124 for four. My mouth had dried up a little. There was a small swarm of butterflies doing aerobatics in my stomach. I was wearing my game-face, as sternly serious as I could make it. I didn't pass my new partner on the way to the crease. He was leaning on his bat at the Radcliffe Road end. He nodded a greeting to me, and I nodded one back at him.

It was Ian Bell.

An over or two later, he got a delivery that wasn't too full or too wide of off stump. The front foot went forward, as elegantly as a ballet step. He leant into the ball and drilled it through the covers. It was one of those shots that you know, as soon as it hums off the middle, that the fielder isn't there to stop the ball, but merely to bring it back to the bowler from the boundary the way a dog would fetch a stick.

For me, it could have been 2005 all over again ... except that I was now part of the action instead of watching it from the sofa.

MY DAD MADE a single appearance for England against Australia. It was the Centenary Test at Lord's in 1980. His 29th birthday fell on the fourth day. He accepted that the occasion was much better than the game, which ended tamely in a draw after the weather, showing no respect for a nostalgic anniversary, repeatedly got in the way of the play. The rain swallowed up so many hours of the match that the draw soon became the only outcome. He took two catches and claimed a stumping too. My dad was proud of that. He was also proud that three other Yorkshiremen were on the field beside him: Geoffrey Boycott, Bill Athey and Chris Old. He thought it demonstrated Yorkshire's integral part in so much of what had gone before in the Ashes.

There'd always been an appreciation of history in his approach to the game. Introduced to any former pro, he'd want to know what their era had been like and how it was markedly different from his own. My mum says that he could 'talk cricket all night', and he always sought out those who liked to do the same. Meeting and mingling with more than 200 former England and Australia players was for him like being whisked off in a time machine and finding himself blissfully in the past. He was aware that there were men at the black-tie dinners and the drinks parties, the dressing-up parts of a week-long celebration, whom he would never

meet again once the match was over, such as Stork Hendry, who'd figured in the 1921 Ashes series here, and Percy Fender, who'd gone down there the winter before. He spoke to whomever he could.

As part of an event that was unrepeatable, my dad called the Centenary Test one of his cricketing 'highlights' and also one of the 'great experiences of my life', treasuring the souvenirs he picked up from it. He remembered Old lifting the spinner Ray Bright into the well of the Tavern to avoid the follow-on. And he remembered Kim Hughes returning the insult, straight-hitting Old for six on to the top tier of the pavilion.

I'd already played in eight Tests before I got to Nottingham in 2013, but I discovered there what my dad found out 33 years before me. Nothing compares to a Test against Australia. You feel more than a hundred years of the Ashes pressing down on you like a physical weight, but what really sets the series apart is the sense that everyone is watching – especially, because of 2005, those who aren't motivated to follow a Test against anyone else. Patriotism pulls them towards the Ashes. So it's like walking on to a stage with every light on and turned up to full beam. You're in the glare of things like never before.

The thrill of opening day of the opening Ashes Test is different from any other. You sing 'God Save the Queen' for the first time. You get – as we did at Trent Bridge – the Red Arrows roaring above you, the sky suddenly streaked with a smoky trail of red, white and blue, which lingers a while before breaking into wispy strands. You look around and see the flag unfurled everywhere, rippling across each of the popular stands in high waves. It was like the Last Night of the Proms. You half expected Elgar to turn up and shake you by the hand.

The scene and the background music prickled the hairs on the back of my neck. Like me, Joe Root was making his Ashes debut. He admitted afterwards that the pomp and circumstance and stagey formalities 'flustered' him. So I can only imagine how the Australians must have reacted – however stoic each of them pretended to be.

The debates and opinions that are traded before an Ashes Test seem ceaseless, making it a relief when the only word that matters is 'heads' or 'tails'. Alastair Cook, after calling correctly, was soon steering a ball off his legs. I remember it gathered speed through mid-wicket as it bumped over the old pitches.

We were off and running.

THE TEST WAS acknowledged as a modern classic, as though drawn from the same vintage as 2005. What happened to me was this: Ian Bell and I racked up a half-century stand. I went on to make 37 in an hour and a half before I drove at – and missed – a full ball from Mitchell Starc, fuming with myself for doing so. In the second innings, on 15, I fell to the left-arm spin of Ashton Agar, a name that, as someone remarked, sounded 'like a village in rural Somerset'.

There was barely a slow moment in the entire game, which for those who saw it became the gift that kept on giving: 14 wickets on the first day ... the obscure Agar, an 18-year-old number eleven who batted like a 30-year-old number four ... the last-wicket partnership he shared with Phil Hughes in the first innings, bringing him 98 and Australia 163 improbable runs ... a typically elegant Ian Bell century in response to it ... and then a fluctuating fifth day of monumental tension.

We were convincingly on top. So much so that it seemed the only thing even the most obsessive punter could sensibly bet on was the exact hour and minute of our win. Needing 311, the Australians were rocking and about to tilt over on 231 for nine, still a continent away from our total. In came the pace bowler James Pattinson, joining Brad Haddin. No doubt some watching at home switched off the TV and went into the garden to top up their tan, expecting the game to last a few more overs at best, unaware that Pattinson had previously made two Test fifties and come close to getting two more. We waited nonetheless for what we were sure was on the way: the nick, a mistiming born out of pressure, the momentary loss of concentration from either of them that would start our party. But then, picking off the runs, Haddin and Pattinson began to slice away at our lead one slither at a time, making the impossible suddenly look feasible for them. The runs piled up incrementally. I looked at the scoreboard, scarcely able to credit that we were straining to get them out. Australia began to close in on us, the deficit almost in single figures. I can sense the atmosphere of a match as it changes as surely as I can feel a wind that abruptly starts blowing in a different direction. I became aware of the quiet unease that had settled over Trent Bridge.

Jimmy Anderson has bowled thousands of deliveries more accurate and accomplished than the one that came next. It wasn't a peach at all. The ball was slightly wide, which made it slightly inviting as well. Haddin went after it. I was at backward point, close enough to hear exactly what the slips heard as he wafted loosely at it. The inside edge was no more than a scratch. The ball began to die, losing so much height as it travelled towards Matt Prior that he finally took the catch in front of his left toecap. Our shout was long and throaty, a plea as much as an appeal. Not out, said the umpire. No review is ever completed quickly nowadays; every angle from every machine is studied the way a pathologist studies a bloodstain. It felt as though half a day had dragged by before the decision of the third umpire eventually arrived. Hot Spot had found the smallest of white smudges. We'd squeaked home, the margin only 14 runs.

You're always being asked how you'd felt as a game or performance was in progress. It's a natural question to put to someone, but it is a difficult one to answer coherently and with any sort of originality. You tend to stumble into platitudes, relying on words like joy or elation, fulfilment or satisfaction because immediately afterwards those are the emotions that are still coursing right through you, like a charge, and also because describing them can be as hard as describing the taste of water. I can only say – in the moment when we knew we'd won – that what I felt was something more intense than I'd ever felt on a cricket ground before. It was ecstasy, undiluted. You can see it in a series of photographs that were taken with a long lens from the Radcliffe Road end of the ground, each cropped into a landscape of most of the team. Put them together and turn each one rapidly, as if you're thumbing the pages of an old-fashioned child's flick book, and you'll see us all dance and run and leap. There are seven of us in the best of these photos. At the back of the group Steve Finn, at 6 foot 7, looks as though he's mastered the art of levitation – he seems at least four feet off the ground. Alastair Cook is seen side-on, jumping into the air and punching it simultaneously. Kevin Pietersen's arms are aloft, like a boxer who's got a unanimous title decision. The others – me, Joe Root and Stuart Broad – are already in pursuit of Jimmy, whose first reaction is to run off to wherever his legs will carry him; it doesn't matter where. His head is back. He's staring up at the sky. He's taken another five-for. I'm closest to Jimmy, but I can't slap him on the back or yank at his shirt to slow him down. He's too quick for me.

Anyone who wants to know how much the Ashes mean only has to look at this photo. All the evidence you'll ever need is in it.

THE FIGHT HAD lived up to the hype at Trent Bridge. Public interest in the series took off from there as though someone had flicked a lighted match into a box of rockets. And, on the first morning of the second Test at Lord's, I saw a sight that I'll never forget because of it.

I went into the dressing-room loo, where I slid back a small window that gives you a view overlooking the Grace Gates and the road that runs along the high perimeter wall, which was built when W.G. was still in knickerbockers. For a long time I stood gazing at the scene below me. There were two rivers in London that day and one of them flowed outside Lord's. The queue, three to four deep in places, ran from the entrance to the tall hotel that stands at the corner of St John's Wood Road and Wellington Road. That's a distance of almost 400 yards. The MCC membership was conspicuous, wearing blazers and hats emblazoned in that sun-bright egg-and-bacon livery or carrying bags on which the silhouette of Father Time always has his sickle slung over his right shoulder. I thought about some of them, getting up at dawn, their eyes still heavy with sleep, and then travelling mile upon mile to secure at all costs a decent seat in the pavilion.

Again, we won the toss. Again, we batted. Again, I came in when we were in the mire – 127 for four. And again, Ian Bell was waiting for me. The Test is prominent in my scrapbook for two very contrasting reasons. The first owed everything to good fortune. The second was quirky and had nothing much to do with the cricket itself.

I started comfortably enough, determined to build an innings that would last, while allowing Ian to do what he always did best, which was to impress everyone with a flourishing shot or two and shake up the Australians, who to me already looked worried about his form; he seemed to have carried it with him from Nottingham as easily as clothes in a suitcase. I'd made a not-bad 21 when I played around a full ball from Peter Siddle. It hit off and middle. Siddle wagged his finger in the air and the fielders gathered to hug him. I slinked away, cursing myself. I'd gone as far as a third of the way to the pavilion gate when the umpire Kumar Dharmasena shouted: 'Wait there,' as though he'd just found something I'd left behind at the crease and was about to ask me to go back for it. His colleague was checking the TV replay, he said.

Only 18 months earlier, during our tour of India, I'd made a critical mistake. I'd immediately accepted I was out in Mumbai when my shot – off Pragyan Ojha – flicked the grille of Gautam Gambhir's helmet at silly point before the catch was completed. I was unaware then that I had a Get Out of Jail Free card. The ball ought to have been declared 'dead' after touching the helmet. I took off my gloves and unstrapped my pads and went into the gym alone to go over my innings. I was angry with myself for the slackness of the shot. I was angrier still after Joe Root appeared, telling me that I shouldn't have been given out. 'We've seen it again on screen. You might still be in,' he told me. Andy Flower asked the match referee to reverse the decision. He was told that, since I'd voluntarily 'walked', India would have to withdraw their appeal first. Their captain MS Dhoni refused, which I guess is the decision we'd have made in the same circumstances. I blamed myself. If I'd known the minutiae of the laws – as I should have done – I'd have refused to budge.

At Lord's my eyes had been pinned on to the ball. I was too busy watching Siddle's hand to register where his front foot had landed. Also, after Trent Bridge – where the Australians had bowled 11 of them – the coach Darren Lehmann had almost made the no-ball a punishable offence for his attack. I didn't expect a reprieve, merely confirmation of my departure, which hanging around in the crease wasn't making easier. I stood there like a spare part, a man in the wilderness unsure of what to do or say. If you'd asked me to calculate my chances as a percentage, I'd have estimated them as ten or fifteen at best. But the all-seeing eye of the camera rescued me. The heel of Siddle's boot was a cat's whisker in front of the line – the margin of error so close that, before technology, no umpire would have spotted it. Even the TV cameras replayed it five times to be absolutely certain. Dharmasena beckoned me back. Siddle, his features gurning in an expression of abject misery, stomped away to his mark.

After the injustice I'd suffered in India, I like to think a sort of cricketing karma had taken place. Ian Bell and I scored exactly 100 more runs before I was finally out for 67. Next morning, the Australians didn't gripe about the decision to go to the third umpire, but did complain that Siddle's millimetre misjudgement could cost them the Test, the series and the Ashes. Originally the claim came across as a bit screeching and melodramatic, but you can argue a case for it now. Our partnership bolted the middle order together – Ian finished on 109 – and we moved from a precariously dodgy position to a secure one. We gave our attack something substantial to bowl at and then we cleaned Australia up. We went on to win the Test – by a whopping 347 runs.

And the quirky reason why the Test was memorable for me? Another photograph.

Get picked for an Ashes Test at Lord's and you know you're going to meet the Queen. She arrived before the start and we lined up for inspection like the household cavalry on Horse Guards Parade. You make sure your hands and fingernails are clean. You think about what she might say to you, and also the small talk you might trade in return. You try to be casual about the experience. I was standing, hands behind my back like Prince Philip, at the end of the row between Ian, who is two inches shorter than I am, and Steve Finn, who is six inches and a bit taller than me. We looked like the gradual incline of an Alpine range. Alastair Cook, smart in his blazer, was a step and a quarter behind the Queen, introducing each of us. She held out her white-gloved hand to me, offering a 'wonderful occasion' and a 'very pleased to meet you'. As she went past, her duty over, my eyes swivelled towards the ground to examine her shoes, which were quite high heeled, shiny black and with a long gold buckle. The

colour matched her handbag. Someone snapped a photograph of me. In it – my head bowed and my gaze low – I look as though I am checking out her bum rather than her shoes. The camera lied, but no one would believe it – or my protests afterwards. Elizabeth I would have lopped off the head of anyone giving her a sideways glance that she hadn't encouraged. Elizabeth II was more forgiving, politely ignoring the photo.

At least as far as I'm aware.

AT 2–0 UP we had enough canniness in the team to put down any Australian attempt to fight back. At Old Trafford, where we were well on top, we had to settle for a draw, the pouring rain impossible to beat. At the Riverside, which was a reasonably low-scoring affair, the match was finely balanced on the fourth day. Australia needed 131. We needed their last seven wickets. Six for 20 in 45 balls was how Stuart Broad turned the Test our way. And at the Oval we were so close – requiring 21 from four overs – when bad light fouled up our run chase, denying us what would have been a stonking – and unprecedented – 4–0 win in the series.

I was only at the Oval briefly on the first day and then again for the last two. In between I ironically found myself back where that Ashes summer began, appearing for Yorkshire in the Championship at Trent Bridge. With the rubber won, and with a thought or two towards the forthcoming winter in Australia, England decided to make three changes. I wasn't so much dropped as handed a leave of absence. One moment I was in the England nets, the start of the game barely two hours away, the next I was hurtling towards Nottingham. My mum and Becky were hurtling there too, travelling from Headingley with my Yorkshire gear in the boot of the car. Becky was driving because mum was too ill. When I reflected on missing out at the Oval, and also on the Tests I'd played in, I was annoyed only because I knew I'd done enough to go to Australia but hadn't made the big score – a century or more – that would have established me properly.

The winter tour would be the fourth Ashes series in four and a half years; we were getting to know the Australians almost as well as our own families. I'd been to the country only once before. In 2010 I had been chosen for the England Performance Programme. Like most long-distance travel, it's slightly a surprise when you actually get there, but a month and a half spent in Brisbane and Perth sticks in the mind not so much for the cricket as for the friendship I forged.

I'd first come across James Taylor when we played opposite one another in a schools' competition. We weren't yet teenagers. Not long afterwards we faced one another again. He was scrum-half and I was fly-half in a rugby match. James is only 5 foot and a handful of inches, so with great unoriginality we called him Titch. He and I are similar personalities and we share almost identical interests, which enabled us to room together for three years. On tour you live in one another's pockets and connect with everyone back home regularly on Skype. So I got to know his mates and also his family, and he got to know mine. We spoke a lot about everything, and so often were we seen in one another's company that we became known as 'Mr and Mrs'. In Brisbane, the two of us even shared an apartment. It turned out to be more men behaving untidily than badly. We split the core chores between us: I would cook; he would clean. This was a sensible division of labour. I'm no chef, but I soon learnt Titch's culinary skills were so rudimentary that he made me seem cordon bleu and multi-Michelin-starred. At one point, unsure about how to heat up beans, he whacked the tin in the microwave and switched it on. I'm not sure he even opened the tin first.

I found I liked Australia the way my dad had done. He felt at home there and agreed with the view that most Australians are actually Yorkshiremen in disguise, our two tribes so alike that not much separates Skipton from Sydney or Mexborough from Melbourne except better weather and twelve thousand miles. We're equally tough, equally competitive, equally stubborn and equally willing to talk to whoever is in the same bar as us.

The forecasts for the series were good to very good for us. We felt we possessed the upper hand psychologically. We'd lost only two of the previous fifteen Tests against Australia. Essentially the same in-form team that had beaten them here was now going there and could afford to draw, if necessary. Our leading players had made almost 500 Test appearances between them. I thought we were a disciplined, tough lot and I sensed no complacency either. Most of those among us – Alastair Cook, Kevin Pietersen, Jimmy Anderson, Stuart Broad, Graeme Swann and Matt Prior, for example – knew what it took to win in Australia, having done it barely two years earlier when the sprinkler dance was born in celebration. We also had Jonathan Trott and Ian Bell and the pro's pro, Tim Bresnan, each of them veterans of that 2010–11 triumph. There was Joe Root too. And age would hardly weary us. The gap between the Oval and the first Test in Brisbane was only 101 days, the first rubber to be held back to back with the previous one for almost four decades.

The onus was on the Australians. And so was the pressure. The only strike bowler who could conceivably come in to strengthen them was Mitchell Johnson. It seemed like an awfully big adventure for us and a trial for them.

What could possibly go wrong?

CHAPTER 8

ARE YOU HERE FOR ALL THE TESTS?

THE ASHES SERIES that root themselves in the memory – even for those of us who weren't there – almost always pivot around a bowler so devastatingly quick that he dominates it, his influence the difference between the teams.

You don't have to be much of a historian to know that, either. Go back as far as 1882 and the Demon Spofforth, the first man to seriously eyeball a batsman in an attempt to unsettle him. His gaze is supposed to have been as horrifying as the Gorgon's. He finished with match figures of 14 for 90 at the Oval, reducing England to rubble. Think of Bodyline in 1932–33 when, against Harold Larwood, the Australians – including Don Bradman – were advised to kiss their wives and insure their lives before going out, as though heading into a war zone. The opener Bill Brown, about to face the MCC in a State game, remembered that he lay awake at night, wondering how he'd defend himself with a heavy bat and fearing that Larwood would kill him. Think also of Frank Tyson, who according to Richie Benaud 'absolutely smashed' Australia in 1954–55, taking 28 wickets. And think of 1974–75, that Down Under summer when Jeff Thomson and Dennis Lillee were petrifyingly fast.

Since the grisly highlights of that series have been shown so often, we can recall in a flash the seminal image from them: Thomson attempting to rearrange David Lloyd's genitals – the ball coming off the bare pitch, thumping into his box and then poor Bumble almost folded in half in pain so obviously excruciating that you almost feel it yourself. On that tour the infirmary became a regular port of call for the batsmen. There were broken ribs and pulverised fingers and thumbs, and also the sort of body bruising that you'd suffer after being beaten up in a back alley. In a postscript Mike Denness, the England captain, said candidly: 'I don't think the public or the media will ever appreciate what the players went through on that tour … we had encountered a new dimension in speed.' Some batsmen, he added, went home 'relieved' to have avoided 'fatal injury'.

In 2013–14, almost 40 years on, we could say something along similar lines.

Robert Louis Stevenson once wrote that it can be 'better to travel hopefully than to arrive', which is sound advice from someone who shipwrecked his most famous character in a storm, leaving him to get by almost, but not quite, on his tod. I know what Stevenson meant. We travelled hopefully to Australia, favourites to win a fourth successive Ashes series – something England had not done since the nineteenth century. When we arrived, however, we hit the storm. Its name was Mitchell Johnson.

With 37 wickets at 13.97, Johnson reached the sunlit peak of his career. At 32 years old, he found an extraordinary flush of form that no one will ever forget – even if, like me, you'd prefer to. His was the golden arm, and he gave a once-in-a-generation performance with it. He wasn't only man of the series; he *was* the series, bracketed afterwards beside Spofforth and Larwood, Tyson and Thomson and Lillee. Johnson portrayed himself beforehand as a villain, promising that he'd go for our 'throat'. He looked the part too. The droop of that gaucho moustache made him resemble a gun-slinging cowboy from one of those spaghetti westerns of the 1960s and 1970s. All he needed, as he ran in to bowl, was his own sinisterly haunting Ennio Morricone soundtrack ...

To be whitewashed because of Johnson – suffering only the third 5–0 defeat in 131 years of the Ashes – was humiliating enough for us. But the collateral damage, spreading from the epicentre of the havoc he caused, had consequences that seemed far-fetched before the series started but understandable afterwards. Andy Flower resigned as coach as soon as the tour was over. Jonathan Trott, citing a stress-related illness, went home as soon as the first Test had finished. Graeme Swann quit international cricket before the fourth Test. Seven other members of the party who figured during that series haven't been seen in a Test since. One of them was Kevin Pietersen. Even Matt Prior played in only another four matches for England before his retirement. Johnson changed the entire look of our team. I'm certain, given the unstoppable ferociousness of his pace, that he'd have done the same to any side at any time. We just happened to be in absolutely the wrong place at absolutely the wrong time.

I thought about my dad, who was part of one particular tour that he described as 'horrendous'. It began badly for him and barrelled downhill at an awful pace from there. In 1981 he went to the West Indies as number-one wicket-keeper, but came back as deputy to Paul Downton. He'd barely unpacked, let alone practised, before he missed two stumpings on a hard, erratic pitch. He went in as night-watchman and was out for a second-ball duck, which cost him his Test place. He got a rollicking from his captain, Ian Botham, and gave him a rollicking back. This was still a thousand fathoms from his low point.

This was the tour – lost 2–0 – that got caught up in polit-ical controversy because of Robin Jackman's connections

with South Africa, which led to the cancellation of the second Test. This was the tour in which a spectator – who also happened to be a policeman – threatened Geoffrey Boycott with a whitewashed brick. Upset by an lbw decision, Boycs threw a glass of water out of the dressing-room window and soaked the man accidentally. And this was the tour when my dad got to know and appreciate the ex-England and Surrey batsman Ken Barrington, so dearly loved as a player's man and everyone's favourite kindly uncle. You hear about Barrington and get the sense of someone so wonderfully eager about everything, so constantly cheerful on your behalf. Barrington was christened 'Colonel Malaprop' because malapropisms became his trademark. These included:

'There's a lot of bridges to flow over the water yet.'
'I kipped really well. I slept like a lark.'
'That was a great performance in anyone's cup of tea.'

He discovered piña coladas in the West Indies, but couldn't get his tongue around the pronunciation of it, ordering for my dad a 'Peter Granadas' instead, which confused the barman.

Aware that my dad was down in the dumps, and aware too that his relationship with the management had slowly cracked, Barrington regularly sought him out. He took him for personal practice and generally jollied him along, trying to make things better. He was a mediator and a go-between for my dad, but also someone with whom he could relax and speak freely, aware that his trust would never be broken.

The sad nadir of the tour came unexpectedly. One morning, midway through a Test, the England team awoke to discover that Barrington had died of a heart attack the night before. Like everyone else, my dad blubbed his eyes out. No one wanted to go on, but the team did so nonetheless in Barrington's memory. What happened on that tour was catastrophic compared to my own experience, but I still knew a little of what my dad meant afterwards when remembering it. He said he felt throughout as though he was 'a long way from home'.

YOU TEND TO forget – because what happened over the next five weeks shrank it to a footnote – that Australia were teetering on 132 for six on the first day of the first Test at Brisbane, where the air was humid and the sun desert-hot. Stuart Broad had skittled out the top order, taking four of them for not much. The mood only fundamentally shifted when Mitchell Johnson came in to partner Brad Haddin.

The statistics of his 64 don't exactly jump off the page: 143 minutes; 134 balls; 6 fours; 2 sixes. But what I remember, sitting on the balcony, is the mood music that went with those figures. Australia had been reeling, as if from a surprise punch, but Johnson's conviction that he could steady them again – and then begin a fight-back – transmitted itself from him to the crowd, who so far had been fairly muted. He biffed a few balls around, rousing them out of their despondency. When he biffed a few more, you heard the chant of his Christian name, which became so familiar. It was chopped into two syllables – 'Mit-chell'.

This fog-horn drone spread across the ground. More than 30,000 Queensland spectators responded to a fellow Queenslander, and Johnson responded to them, each feeding off the raw energy of the other. He never looked back. We lost the Test by 381 runs. Johnson took four for 61 in the first innings and five for 42 in the second. His series took off in a fantastic burst of action because of it. At Adelaide, even though the surface was slower than Brisbane, we got bundled out for 172. Johnson took the first wicket. He then claimed the last six, the batsmen making only nine between them. At least in the second innings he spared us the rod, taking only one wicket, as though saving himself for later on. Australia won by 218 runs.

And so it went on …

At Perth, where the defeat this time was 150 runs, Johnson had match figures of six for 140 and Australia claimed the Ashes back more than a week before Christmas.

Johnson called the series his 'redemption', admitting in retrospect that if he'd trudged away from it with 'my tail between my legs', he'd have been 'written off as a cricketer' forever more. He knew, too, that a lot of critics had written him off anyway and were wondering how he'd got back in the team. His mental toughness was under scrutiny. His fitness was questioned too; he'd made only three Test appearances in 12 months since returning from South Africa, where he'd limped away with a toe injury, and the selectors had overlooked him for the tour to England. This was a now-or-never comeback for him. Johnson was aware that, English and Aussie alike, you can play twelve dozen Tests against anyone else in the world, but be defined only by what you achieve in the Ashes. He'd also been considerably narked about – and never forgotten – the Barmy Army's comic song, which mocked him during the 2010–11 series. The lyrics, though not quite to the emotional standard of a Lennon and McCartney ballad, did have a certain swing to them, I suppose.

> *He bowls to the left, he bowls to the right.*
> *That Mitchell Johnson, his bowling is shite.*

No wonder he bowled as if we pissed him off simply by being there.

Johnson insisted he was such a 'nervous wreck' before the first Test that he almost called for a pair of brown corduroy trousers. But he set out to bowl fast. 'If I can't, I don't want to bowl at all,' he'd said. His first ball of the series – full, wide and harmless – was clocked at just under 90 mph. At Adelaide he reached 93.5 mph. Elsewhere, he nudged 95 mph. So it wasn't simply that Johnson went up a gear against us; he seemed to have found a whole new propulsion system within him – a warp drive. As well as being more aggressive than I'd ever seen him, he was also more accurate, making it difficult even to push away a run. And, rather than bowling sustained spells, he was rested and then released at us fresh in a boom that lasted only three overs at a time but reverberated long afterwards, the way a rumble of thunder lingers in the air.

Jonathan Trott called Johnson his 'executioner'. What he had, said Trott, was 'steep bounce … from a length that other people couldn't replicate'. He was also more assured and controlled than before. 'A different man' was how Trott put it. Kevin Pietersen went further. He was, explained KP, 'a different bloke entirely'. He was 'in our heads even when he wasn't bowling' and became 'a weapon that we had no answer to'. KP felt 'a shudder' shoot through the dressing room early on in Brisbane when Johnson, bowling to Trott, let one go so violently that only a glove stopped the bumper from smacking into the grille of the helmet.

I reached Australia not expecting to get into the Test team unless something extraordinary happened. I was there as a 12th-man type – fetching drinks, carrying towels, tidying up the dressing room, practising in the nets. I remained fairly anonymous to the Australian public too. In the beginning, I could walk around without being recognised. If I only wore my England tracksuit top or T-shirt, everyone assumed I was another supporter, a member of the Barmy Army. 'You here for all the Tests?' someone asked me in a shop. 'Hope so,' I replied, saying nothing more.

The only barracking came when Gary Ballance and I shipped out to Perth for a match with the England Performance XI. With our conspicuously big bags covered in ECB logos, we were unmistakably cricketers on the move and not fans there to soak up the sun. When we reached our hotel, a group of workers on a neighbouring construction site turned the air blue with a flamethrower blast of insults, dire warnings about our chances of survival against the Aussie bowlers and an invitation to book ourselves on the first available flight home.

I'm guessing the construction workers weren't overly impressed with me, but I got a century in that match, which was only my third appearance on tour. The first had come against an Australian Invitational XI in Sydney. I made 48 and claimed seven catches. The second was against the Cricket Australia Chairman's XI in Alice Springs, where I finished with a tidy, unbeaten 30-odd and took a stumping off Graeme Swann. I still wasn't in good fettle. Becky arrived from England, bringing with her another bat, a pair of wicket-keeping gloves and some other kit for me. It took up precious space in the case where more of her clothes should have gone. Not much sisterly intuition was needed to know that I was downcast and out of sorts. I sat in the room and watched her unpack in silence.

The earlier games were useful, but scarcely white-hot preparation for what came next for me. With the Ashes gone, and with Matt Prior off-form, I found myself thrown into the Boxing Day Test, which is a bit like playing in a cup final without experiencing any of the previous rounds.

The Melbourne Cricket Ground rises around you, a great coliseum even when empty. You practise on that vast outfield, picturing what it'll be like when everyone is crammed inside it. When everyone is, there's nothing like it in cricket – the colour, the constant hubbub, the sheer number of fans in those wide, steep tiers, where the topmost rows are lost in shadow when the sun sinks. I can't say I slept much the night before, though not because the Test overawed me. If you don't want to play in a match like this, you shouldn't be a cricketer. My only apprehension stemmed from being ring-rusty and the fact that a place such as Traeger Park in Alice Springs (capacity 10,000) is gorgeously appealing, fringed as it is with low brown hills, but about as different from the MCG as Arundel and Cheltenham are from Lord's. It's no preparation for the grander stage.

As soon as you step into the nets you get an idea of how daunting the atmosphere in the Test will be. There's a balcony overlooking them, enabling those on it to look down on you. It's as though some Roman thumb is about to be jerked upward or downward in judgement. The locals attempt to rile you, the throwaway comments about being 'no-good poms' with 'no chance' being fairly standard. We lost the toss, and Australia made the predictable decision to put us in. You couldn't blame them because of the partisan crowd, waiting for us to buckle again. We made a respectable start. Alastair Cook and Michael Carberry put on almost fifty, and we'd almost doubled that score before the second wicket went down; Johnson didn't take either of them.

I was batting at seven. Sometimes I like to doze before I go out. I have the knack of being able to nod off in most places at most times. The old-school rule says that you should watch every ball and be aware of what every bowler is doing with it, but that was laid down in the era well before you were able to swot up on anyone, replaying any delivery from a multitude of angles with a few clicks of a laptop mouse. In the dressing room, I'll lay a thick towel on the hard floor or across the bench, and stretch myself out for a while. I once nodded off sitting down – my head forward, my hands on the handle of my bat as I pressed them against my forehead. I find a quick nap relaxing. I don't take long, a minute perhaps, to snap awake, and I feel alert afterwards.

My dad was the same. Once, he snoozed in the dressing room at Scarborough, which is difficult enough because the spectators are right outside the door. He woke up without realising that a run chase, arranged beforehand, had been called off while he'd been sleeping. No one thought to tell him. He came out intent on causing mayhem with the bat. At the other end, his partner, stonewalling for a draw, looked completely nonplussed as my dad began trying to win the match with some whirlwind hitting. The *Yorkshire Post* wrote that 'Bairstow flailed away like a man demented until someone plucked up the courage to explain the reality of the situation to him'.

I didn't sleep before going out at Melbourne. The atmosphere, the state of the game and the prospect of what Johnson might do kept my eyes open. Wide open, in fact. You don't come across too many bowlers as fast as he is.

Fewer still who are left-arm (England have never had a left-armer who's taken 100 Test wickets).

With his sling-shot action, Johnson's arm disappears behind his back just before he delivers the ball. He's like a magician hiding the trick. You see the ball so late that you have no idea where it's going until the thing is well on its way. This is the exact opposite of facing someone such as Dale Steyn. You can clearly see the ball – as well as his wrist position and how his fingers are gripping the seam – because Steyn's hand is beside his face as he launches into his delivery stride. You have a fraction longer, about half a heartbeat, to size up the line and length.

We were on 202 for four and the ball was relatively new when Johnson, close to the stumps, got one to go away from Ben Stokes for his first wicket, an edge taken at slip. When someone is out, there's usually silence in the dressing room. I picked up my bat, only half-registering a 'good luck' said in a way that implied 'don't get hurt'. The winding walk from dressing room to crease seemed as long as trekking from John o' Groat's to Land's End. There were wide corridors to navigate and I had plenty of time to think. I turned a corner and found myself walking past the members, some of whom weren't slow to offer the opinion that I would be walking past them again in 'less than five minutes'. Ahead I saw the field in the harsh wash of light, and also the hard roof-lines of the stands. Once you're in full view, you look around and blink your eyes to get them accustomed to the brightness as the noise of the place rolls towards you.

Johnson was already at the start of his run, rubbing the ball against his flannels, his expression set into a mask of menace and indignation. The introduction of the stump microphone has reduced the amount of sledging in Tests – everyone is wary about a fine – but the fielders, especially the slips, chuntered away, the conversations coming my way. The talk was about how Johnson's tail was *really* up now. About how his bowling had suddenly caught alight and he was ready to burn through me and what was left of us, leaving only cinders. You're always braced for this yackety-yak, the attempt to take the battle into your mind before it starts on the pitch. Johnson contributed to it himself. He made a show of waving in a short leg and a leg gully and then he pushed a fielder back on to the long-leg boundary. I was left to decide whether this was an elaborate con, the preparation for a yorker, or a very short ball that I'd either have to fend down, sway away from or be courageous enough to hook.

There were three deliveries left in the over. The first of them wasn't dug in at all. Johnson angled it across me and I let it go through on a length, comfortably shouldering arms as if it was the most natural thing to do. The second came at me from halfway down the pitch, and I saw it early, ducking lower than I needed to go but listening to the hum and swish of the seam through the air as it passed half a mile overhead and into Brad Haddin's gloves. The third brought me runs. The ball was outside off and fuller than Johnson had planned. It was there to be driven, so I went for it and ran for a couple through extra cover. I'd survived the first onslaught, much to the crowd's chagrin.

Johnson once compared playing at the MCG that day to being a rock singer and strutting about the stage in front of a band, each of whom followed his lead. I can see the connection. Normally, I can find Becky, her hair like a warning light, even in capacity crowds. My eyes hunt her out like radar and I know my mum will be in the next seat. I did a sweep of the faces packed in front of me. I couldn't see either of them.

At the end of the over the electronic scoreboard flashed up the attendance figure in big white numbers – 91,092 – and declared it a world record. On screen the cameras then showed a close-up of my face. My expression was as blank as I could make it, betraying nothing, I hoped. Though I didn't know it, Bill Lawry was on commentary. 'His heart will be pumping,' he said, as though he could hear it thumping against my chest.

He wasn't wrong.

MITCHELL JOHNSON AND I weren't strangers.

I'd pitted myself against him before. Indeed, he was partly responsible for getting me back into the England team in 2012. Slap in between the end of the West Indies series and the opening stages of the South Africa one, I'd been picked for England Lions against Australia A at Old Trafford. Johnson took four wickets in the first innings, but in the second I faced him down, making 139 at almost a run a ball. That I did so well, blunting him into the bargain, was sufficient for the selectors. I was recalled for Lord's, able to begin my Test career again after a pause rather than a protracted wait. Manchester, it's fair to say, didn't offer as much to Johnson as the MCG did.

I've never minded fast bowling, mostly because of my dad who came up against a few quicks himself. He once belted Dennis Lillee back over his head for six and got a reply comprising almost every known expletive – some of them barked twice, apparently. My dad, unafraid of the bouncer reprisals to come, took a step down the pitch and calmly suggested that, rather than 'chuntering on', Mr Lillee ought to 'go fetch the ******* ball' so he could bowl at him again.

He wasn't always on the winning side, however. He got banged over the eye so badly in a Roses match that a doctor put stitches into the cut while he was still on the field. In another match – thankfully he was wearing a helmet – he got a blow on the left side of his head. The swelling immediately became an egg-sized lump, his ear began to bleed and he was so dizzy for days afterwards that medical advice sidelined him for more than a week. The last Test match of his career took place in Barbados, during that ill-fated tour, where he watched close-up what's been tagged as The Greatest Over of All Time. In the scorebook, it's innocently recorded as: *G Boycott b Holding 0*. On YouTube – though the clip is rather grainy – you appreciate why those six balls are recalled with gasps. Whispering Death? You bet. Michael Holding, beautiful in his action, sent down what was 'a loosener' to him but would be considered as lightning by anyone else. The ball rose, rapped Boycs on the gloves and nearly carried to first slip. The second delivery beat him outside off stump. The third struck him on the inside of the right leg. The fourth and fifth were somehow defended with the body.

On a warm day, the Barbados Oval had swelled beyond capacity. Spectators had lapped on to the boundary's edge; some were even sitting on the thin galvanised roofs of the stands. The crowd knew Holding was cranking up his pace. Each ball bowled was faster than the one before. The sixth ball was an incandescent blur. Boycs's off stump was gone, uprooted and cartwheeling like a matchstick flicked casually from someone's fingers. You have to say that very few batsmen could have survived even as long as Boycs did. Some, afraid of the physical danger, would have backed away waving the white flag. Boycs being Boycs – and despite being 41 years old then – stood his ground, only beaten by something otherworldly. Given the status of this over in cricket's history, my dad's contention that Holding bowled even faster on the second morning in the final Test in Jamaica – he pushed himself off from the boundary wall with the sole of his right boot – makes you wish there'd been a speed gun to provide clinching evidence of it.

Some of the early instruction my dad gave me was based around speed. There wasn't much of that 'give it some loop' stuff from him to me, perhaps because of Holding and Lillee and the rest. Sometimes my uncle Ted reminds me about how he bowled to me with a cork ball. I was about four years old, and he began twisting deliveries out of the side of his hand or lobbing them underarm. The ball would drift so slowly that it took an age to get to me. I'd take a few swipes, hopeless air shots. 'Bowled you,' he'd shout, the noise of his triumph reaching my dad, who bustled over eager to see what the fuss was about. He watched Uncle Ted beat me again before asking, in a bit of a huff, what the heck was going on. He grabbed the ball and said: 'That's not the way you bowl at him.'

My uncle Ted stood back and watched my dad wind himself up like a baseball pitcher or someone wanting to win a coconut at the fair. He flung the ball at me with terrific speed. Uncle Ted had troubling believing what he saw. The boy who couldn't pick the softest dollydrop was transformed, 'whacking the ball everywhere', he said. There were drives off the back as well as the front foot. There were cuts and pulls too. 'Proper, grown-up strokes,' he added, eyes widening as my dad chucked the ball faster still at me.

Len Hutton, who didn't have the benefit of a helmet, once said that the best place to play a fast bowler is from 'the non-striker's end', which is a short-term plan but not a sustainable strategy. Hutton thought something else too: anyone who claimed not to be a little 'afraid of being hit' was either telling a fib to others or wasn't being honest with himself. Hutton had a point. I don't mind admitting that facing Johnson did make me a little afraid too; every nerve in your body is aware of what could happen.

My innings lasted 19 minutes. Out of 17 deliveries, a dozen of them were against Johnson. The highlight – if you can call it that – was a six. I'd like to say that I drove the ball back over his head. Or that I hooked him savagely into the crowd behind square. Or even that I leaned back and cut audaciously to deep backward point. My shot wasn't that slick or attractive, I'm afraid. I swung across the line of a half-tracker. The ball came off the top edge and took an almighty flight, which was another sign of Johnson's terrific pace. It sailed over my head ... over the head of Brad Haddin, who leapt instinctively for it but would have needed to be 30 feet tall to take a catch ... and then over the boundary rope, dropping a foot in front of the sightscreen directly behind.

Like me, Johnson wasn't sure at first about where the shot had gone. His gaze swivelled like the turret of a tank before finding the arc of the ball in the most unlikely place. He gave me a half-grin, as though he wasn't sure whether a choice remark or a stony sort of pity would better convey his contempt of my effort. I was gone two balls later, dismissed for 10. The delivery was full and fast and went across me and between bat and pad. Johnson did what every fast bowler aims to do; he clipped the top of off stump. I realised – but only after I saw the recording – that I'd dragged my back foot to leg; I looked a fool.

After every wicket, Johnson had been high-fiving his Australian teammates. He did so only half-heartedly after getting me out. He concentrated instead on giving a wave to the England supporters – or specifically to a group of them, gathered not far from third man, who'd been 'a bit chatty', he said. He thought my wicket would 'shoosh' them up a bit. I was one of five batsmen he got rid of in only eight overs, hustling us out for 255. We lost the match by eight wickets and I fell to him in the second innings too; though at least I made 21 and also claimed six catches in the match.

Reflecting about *that* over against Holding, Boycs said pointedly: 'For the first time in my life, I can look at a scoreboard with a duck against my name and not feel a profound sense of failure.' I didn't feel a sense of failure against Johnson either. It was a defeat, but an honourable one. None of us had anything but fleeting success against Johnson, usually a pyrrhic victory, before he claimed our wicket or softened us up, allowing someone else to take it. In the five Tests we only scored six half-centuries and one century, a 120 that Ben Stokes managed at Perth.

How do I rate Johnson? Put it this way: when he retired, I thought about sending him a postcard with a message that said: 'Thanks, mate. You've just made all our lives far easier.'

JONNY WILKINSON NEVER forgot what became dubbed The Tour of Hell. In 1998 he and England went to Australasia and South Africa and came back humbled. The trip became one moment of anguish after another for him. There was a 76–0 surrender to Australia in Brisbane. There was a 64–22 loss to New Zealand in Dunedin. Those drubbings were so severe that being beaten 18–0 by South Africa in Cape Town looked almost respectable, like the start of a partial recovery. It still meant that in seven gruesome matches – all defeats – England had conceded a total of 328 points.

Wilkinson said that he 'personally' suffered embarrassment, shame and even a sense of worthlessness because of it. Piling in on top of those emotions came others too – predominantly anger and bitterness, which were sparked by the helplessness and frustration he felt during and after the matches. 'A very bad dream,' he called it, adding that the shock of being roughed up and losing so comprehensively not only made him feel vulnerable, but also scrambled his whole perspective of the tour. 'I just couldn't get a handle on how bad it was. I couldn't absorb it properly right there and then,' he admitted.

There was another confession from Wilkinson. The thought of what had happened reduced him to tears. He only came out of his deep funk after his father, hearing him talk only about yesterday, made him concentrate on tomorrow. 'What are you going to do about it?' he asked. The logic of the question jolted him out of his despair the way a hypnotist's demand to 'wake up' abruptly draws someone out of a trance. What had seemed like the end of something to Wilkinson was immediately transformed into a beginning instead. He saw the tour differently from then on. It became 'a lesson in disguise' and also a 'fork in the road', he said. He stopped feeling sorry for himself. He stopped beating himself up too. He realised that moping would get him nowhere.

Wilkinson accepted the hurt the result had caused him, but also rationalised it and moved on. He used the tour as a spur, a way of motivating himself. The player who already practised tirelessly now spent even longer than before on his drills, his fitness, his focus. Out of his distress came a 'better way' to achieve his goals – and also 'a better goal to strive for altogether', he explained. The tour became one of the most 'valuable experiences' of Wilkinson's life because it hardened him.

We lost the last Test in Sydney by 281 runs. We were mincemeat by the third day. At one point in our first innings we were 23 for five. Our second innings lasted only 31.4 overs, which was pitiful. My series ended with a third-ball duck. I felt then the way that Wilkinson had felt in 1998. And, like him, I went through the same sort of upheavals and doubts because of it, and a period of bleak introspection, the worst I'd ever gone through.

But, also like him, I eventually came out of it – wiser and tougher, a different and better player as a consequence.

CHAPTER 9

TWO PHOTOGRAPHS, TWO ERAS

OFTEN THE SIGNIFICANCE of something slips by and becomes obvious only in retrospect. You look at events in the rear-view mirror and see them suddenly with a clarity that had been absent before. Out of something that, at the time, seemed messed up or jumbled emerges what you recognise in hindsight as a turning point, entirely logical and necessary.

The 12 weeks between the end of that Ashes tour and the build-up towards Yorkshire's County Championship season were the most important of my career – even though I barely played a match. I know that now. I didn't then because I was so tired, so confused and so disillusioned with cricket that I didn't want to go near it. At one point I seriously thought about quitting the game and trying to break into rugby.

It happened like this.

Those months in Australia exhausted me. After the last Test, I felt mentally shot. I wanted nothing more than to come home and take stock quietly, reflecting with a painful slowness on what I'd learnt from the series. But England sent me on the Lions tour of Sri Lanka. The basic plan was sound enough. I hadn't played much over the winter. So surely I'd benefit from more game time, ensuring that I'd be sharper when the new season began here?

From the best possible intentions came the worst possible consequences. As the tour began, I wanted to be anywhere else but Sri Lanka. And, as it continued, I wanted to do anything else but play cricket. It was wretched. I wasn't so much homesick; though, as my dad always did, after spending month upon month in the sun, I'd have loved to have gone for a walk in a hard shower of Yorkshire rain. Knowing that wouldn't happen, I became steadily more dispirited and worn down. Outwardly, at first, I tried to pretend that everything was fine. Inwardly I was in a bad place, not wanting to practise and certainly not wanting to go on to the field.

I roomed, as ever, with James Taylor, who knows me so well that he recognised even before I spoke to him how troubled I'd become. He could see my mood in my face. I was irritable and edgy, the opposite of the friend he knew. Titch did his best to offer support and advice, but he had his own game to focus on and nothing anyone could have said would really have made a difference to me. Somehow – through sheer will, I guess – I came close to getting a couple of half-centuries, and then made a hundred even when my heart wasn't entirely in it. I batted on autopilot. The last five innings were more indicative of how weary and lacklustre I felt. I averaged 15-something from them. I wasn't in the right state of mind to achieve anything better. I came back from Sri Lanka not wanting to watch, read or talk about cricket at all – not even for half an hour.

I brooded over Australia. Questions about what we might have done differently – and also my minor part in it – surfaced constantly. I couldn't stop turning them over in my mind. No one had made a mountainous pile of runs or taken a substantial number of wickets. Kevin Pietersen top-scored with 279, but 120 of those had come in one Test, and only Stuart Broad had taken over 20 wickets.

In two Tests I'd claimed ten catches, missing only one, in Sydney, when a nick off Chris Rogers bisected Alastair Cook and me, each of us waiting for the other to take it. No fielding relationship is more important for a wicketkeeper than the one he has with his first slip. You have to establish a working geometry, settling on the space and angle between your outstretched hand and his. You also have to develop an expert judgement, anticipating what will happen next. You'll hear a clang, like an alarm going off in your head, when you, rather than him, have to dive for a ball. Eventually, you become like an old married couple, so comfortably familiar that you're capable of finishing one another's sentences. But, in Sydney, Cookie and I were practically at the stage of a first date and still getting used to the way the other played. As a wicketkeeper, you're an Aunt Sally. It's in the small print of your job description. If a half-chance goes in and then out of your gloves again, you've dropped a catch. It's your fault when a bowler sprays a ball, barn-door wide, down leg side and you don't stop four byes. When a throw from the boundary lands three yards in front of you, kicks in the rough and shoots towards your shins, you have to take it cleanly otherwise it's your mistake; you haven't tidied up properly.

Like everyone else, I got taken apart in the post mortem in Australia, which began almost as soon as our last wicket fell. My wicketkeeping was criticised, the chance off Rogers cited as an example of my struggle to master my craft. I'd scored fewer than 50 runs in four innings, so I wasn't rated as much of a batsman either – though I'd scarcely batted since September before being called into that Boxing Day Test at Melbourne. I thought I'd managed as well as anyone could. I'd come late to a series already badly lost and into a team already badly demoralised. Even now I have no clue about what I could have done to prepare for that. No one seemed to appreciate one other pertinent detail either: I'd become England's wicketkeeper without having kept for a full season for Yorkshire. In fact, I'd made only 40 first-class appearances as a wicketkeeper for them since my career began four and a half years earlier. No one seemed to have a broad understanding of my circumstances – or set out to find one – but I was still being written off as unworthy of consideration until I proved myself again in the County Championship. I'd never stood in front of a mirror before and seen failure staring back at me. I did now – and I didn't like it.

First Yorkshire, then a friend and finally – though inadvertently – Liam Plunkett came to my rescue.

YORKSHIRE GAVE ME the pre-season off. A friend invited me to the Cheltenham Festival. I was supposed to go there and back in a day, but I stayed for three. There was nothing posh about our trip. I climbed aboard a beery 'charabanc outing' in Leeds and stayed in a bed and breakfast. I drank the odd glass of champagne. I had a few pints of Guinness. I switched off, forgetting all about Australia, Yorkshire and the County Championship. It was a typical boys' outing, a kind of 'what happens in Cheltenham stays in Cheltenham'. I didn't think about picking up a bat or putting on a pair of wicketkeeping gloves. Afterwards I didn't even go to the gym because I didn't want to drag myself there. Instead, continuing my racing theme, I went to the Grand National.

But every holiday must have a full stop. I came back to a practice game against Northamptonshire at Wantage Road, a morning so unlike spring that the early daffodils almost shrank back into the ground for shelter. It was freezing and dank, and I looked at the clouds expecting much more than a clearing shower to arrive and soak us. The modern player at least has modern thermals. In my dad's day, it would have been three T-shirts and a couple of chunky cable-knit sweaters to ward off hypothermia. There were so few spectators, most of them in big coats and mufflers, that I could probably have walked around the ground and introduced myself to everyone in five minutes. If I'm honest, I didn't fancy being there much more than I'd fancied going to Sri Lanka.

Early on the ball went on to some rough concrete and came back so scuffed up that it looked as though a big dog had tried to take a bite out of it. You'll be familiar with the phrase 'swinging it around corners'. Liam Plunkett did more than that. He swung the damaged ball with a boomerang-like curve and at a scary pace. He broke bones: two Northants batsmen went to the X-ray department. He then claimed his hospital hat-trick. One delivery swerved so much down leg side that I had to leap after it, groping for the thing at full length. The ball bashed into the ring finger of my left hand, pushed the nail into the flesh and fractured the bone. Afterwards it ached as though I'd been hit with a claw hammer. The doctor looked at it, took a sharpish intake of breath and said I'd be out for four to six weeks.

He was wrong; I was back in three.

Having not wanted to play before, I now wanted to play very much. First that recreational period away from the game and then the enforced absence from it galvanised me. I was refreshed, which made me relax too. In March I'd dreaded the season to come. In May I couldn't wait for mine to start.

I also decided to change my batting technique. I quietly went into the Yorkshire nets, which are below the East Stand at Headingley. Ian Dews stood beside the bowling machine and fed balls into it for me. My original idea was simply to play straight. Get my balance. Get my head and eyes over the ball. I wanted to stop going after deliveries – and I also wanted to start playing them later rather than in front of me. The change I made was minimal but critical. I stood with a raised backlift, and it felt comfortable. Before anyone else but me, Ian knew it was going to work. I hit one ball so high and hard that it punched a hole in the wall behind him. The ball is still lodged there. I began timing shots so well that Ian thought his job had become dangerous and almost went off to find a suit of armour.

Looming ahead was our Championship match at Durham, which Sky was broadcasting live. I *had* to be there. It was too important to miss. The TV exposure was an early chance to impress England's selectors again. Jason Gillespie disliked picking anyone who was only half-fit. I had to demonstrate to him that my finger had healed. I wheedled myself into a low-key fixture – so low-key that you won't find it in the record books.

If life is a great wheel, turning to bring you back some-times to a place you've been before, then this was a prime example of it. The match was staged at Sedbergh, on the same spot where I'd made my first XI debut for St Peter's School a decade earlier. The weather, cloudy and overcast, was the same too. Rain was closing in, and for an hour it seemed as though it and I were locked in a race. I needed to score as many runs as quickly as possible before the deluge arrived. I managed it, hitting 40-odd, which was sufficient scorebook proof of my fitness, before the game was ruined.

I don't like to set targets. You can put too much pressure on yourself that way. You can't legislate for the ball that rears up unaccountably or stays absurdly low. Or for the umpire who gives you out when you're not. I got the latter at Durham. I made 97, denied a century only because of a dodgy lbw decision. Replays showed that the ball would only have hit stumps that were three feet high. With my new approach ticking along, I still left Durham thinking that the new England coach Peter Moores – another former wicket-keeper – would have seen enough. I thought he'd pencil me in for the first Test against Sri Lanka at Lord's, which was only a month away. I didn't even make the squad. Nor did I get a consoling phone call to explain why or to offer me the odd scrap of encouragement for the rest of the season.

The frozen wilderness isn't a pleasant place to be – especially when your fall into it is so steep. I found myself in an alien and disorientating landscape. In less than six months I'd gone from somewhere – the status of being England's number-two wicketkeeper – to nowhere, cut out of the reckoning. If I'd snatched at five catches in Australia and dropped all of them, I'd have understood the decision. Even if I'd only been 13th man at Lord's, and then sent back to Yorkshire, I'd have appreciated the thinking behind it. But to be excluded completely, as though I'd become instantly irrelevant, seemed inconceivably harsh to me. Once the initial shock wore off, like an anaesthetic, what I felt was a demoralising pain. I tried to rationalise what had happened, but the sense and meaning of it always slipped away from me. England had nursed me through the ranks. I'd appeared in two Ashes series. I was battle-hardened. Why abandon me now?

I began to think my uncle Ted may have been right. Maybe I should have chosen rugby ahead of cricket. Perhaps I could have carved out a better career for myself there. I dwelt –

albeit fairly briefly – on whether, approaching 25, I could still make a late switch. Could I get myself into physical shape and persuade a club to sign me? But then thoughts about 'fight or flight' buzzed into my head again. I've always argued my corner, combatively if necessary; I'm exactly like my dad in that respect. When I was in Yorkshire's academy side, I wanted to know why I wasn't being promoted to the second XI. When I reached the second XI, I wanted to know why I hadn't broken into the first team. But I learnt that, once you've been told the answer, there is nothing to be gained by banging on about it in public. Or by going in a sulk. I decided to say nowt, buckle down and prove England wrong.

That ancient Chinese proverb – how a 'journey of a thousand miles begins with a single step' – usefully sums up the way back I chose. My single step was the decision to go on, persevere and win back a Test place, however long it took. There was just one stage on which I could do that: the County Championship. And I didn't only want to perform so well in it that England couldn't possibly ignore me. I wanted us to win the title too.

MORE THAN EVER we live in a Twenty20, white-ball world. Spectators like it. Television definitely likes it. And players also like it because of the financial bounty, unimaginable even a decade ago. Our careers can be ephemeral, flourishing one moment but over the next through injury, burn-out or loss of form. That's worth remembering when one of us gets accused of greed after heading off to the Indian Premier League or the Big Bash. I belong to the T20 generation. I saw the competition begin, and I've watched it develop, gradually seeping into every nook and cranny of cricket before entirely reshaping the domestic and international calendars. No one before T20 was in the nets sharpening their hand speed or on the edge of the square practising distance-hitting, the ball arcing into the stands like a drive off a golf tee. As for the reverse sweep and the paddle scoop … you wouldn't have dared. You'd have been marked down as stark mad or a cricketing heathen.

T20 was a part of my growing up – and it's been part of my career too – but I've never lost my respect for the County Championship as a consequence. That's because no county is more synonymous with it than Yorkshire, where the trophy and the pennant are almost considered to be family heirlooms. But that's also because of my dad, who considered the Championship to be 'everything' and the 'main reason' why he played. To him it was the ultimate prize as well as the ultimate test of the county pro. His view seems anachronistic nowadays, when the grounds are full for T20 matches and three-quarters empty for Championship games, but every year you only have to look at the celebrations after the title is won to know how much it still matters and also what it means. You sweat through days and weeks and months for it. It's a battle of endurance, a trial physically and mentally to sustain form, confidence, hope and belief.

Those who win the Championship, collecting a silver medal in a box, are proud of it. Those who don't envy them.

My dad, having seen Yorkshire repeatedly crowned champions in the 1960s, dearly wanted a Championship of his own. He never got his wish. He won the John Player League in 1983, a year in which Yorkshire finished at the foot of the Championship for the first time in their history (imagine what my dad thought about *that*). Four years later he won the Benson & Hedges Cup at Lord's. Yorkshire beat Northamptonshire. The scores were level as the last ball was bowled, the win sealed because Yorkshire had lost fewer wickets. He celebrated as though it was Christmas Day, New Year's Eve and the Queen's Jubilee rolled into one. The joy this win brought him was evident in every line of his

face. In a close-up photograph taken of him on the Lord's balcony, you see the spread of crow's feet from his eyes and those curved crevices from his cheekbones to his mouth. They are deeply pronounced because his smile is so wide, so full. I never tire of seeing this picture because my dad is the personification of happiness in it.

He came close to the Championship only once. In 1975, not expecting much from the summer, Yorkshire surprised themselves and everyone else, losing only one match but finishing second – 16 points behind Leicestershire, who were captained by Ray Illingworth. The seasons around that one were often about mid-table finishes or even a drop below it: 10th, 13th, 14th. There was even a 16th place at a time when there were only 17 counties.

The writer Alan Gibson, a man of the South Riding, once said of Yorkshire's disputatious history: 'It's the bugbear of Yorkshiremen that they always have to behave like Yorkshiremen or in their fixed belief of what a Yorkshireman should be: tough, ruthless, brave, mean.' The club my dad fought for throughout the 1970s and 1980s was a demonstration of that statement made flesh.

At its tamest my dad called Yorkshire a 'soap opera'. At its bitterest he alluded to it as a 'tragedy', which summons something of Shakespeare. There was certainly a Shakespearean scale to things at Yorkshire – and many characters were Shakespearean-like – but it would take the amount of paper that Tolstoy ate up publishing a single novel to even outline the full stirring of the plot.

I'll keep this brief.

Geoffrey Boycott took over the captaincy in 1971. He was replaced in 1978 when Illingworth returned to manage the team. My dad believed Illingworth had been brought back to get Boycs out of the dressing room altogether. 'He would have succeeded,' he explained, 'in any other county but Yorkshire.' When Boycs was ousted, the malice in the explanation for it wasn't even thinly disguised. 'It is not for what you have done, but because of what you are,' he was told. Flash forward to 1983. Yorkshire's cricket sub-committee sack Boycs and its general committee award him a testimonial. The contradiction makes no sense, but shows that Yorkshire's politics had become a fractious and tangled weave.

The general committee was 23-strong, elected on a regional basis in 17 different constituencies, stretching alphabetically from Barnsley to York. Each of them, my dad said, had their own, sometimes fiercely independent and idiosyncratic ideas about how Yorkshire ought to be run. Hours of every annual general meeting could be swallowed up by points of order or arcane nitpicking, the business of the team buried beneath it. It annoyed the hell out of my dad. During the climax to a game at Scarborough, one member decided to demonstrate about the issue of 'membership seating'. He parked himself near the sightscreen and periodically disrupted play by moving as the ball was about to be bowled. Yorkshire were closing in on a win, every over vital, but took only nine wickets before the day ended. My dad continually shouted at the protester, urging him to give up. He became convinced afterwards that the man's cussedness, depriving Yorkshire of vital overs, had cost them the match. This stupid incident, long forgotten I imagine, is symbolic of the state of unrest and rebellion that Yorkshire became trapped in.

Civil wars are always the nastiest and the most bloody. Yorkshire proved that.

Some swore by Boycs. Others swore about him. What engulfed Yorkshire in the debate was perpetual controversy: writs, private and public meetings, accusations, recriminations and remorse. Every tongue brought in a tale, and every tale condemned someone as a villain. It became a mudslinging contest – and each side matched the other clod for clod. Politics, personality and pride became more entwined than ever with the cricket. My dad said he 'cringed' to see the club in such a state. It was feeding time for the press, who gorged understandably on every delectable detail. The headlines were gruesome:

YORKSHIRE – THE FAMILY AT WAR
YORKSHIRE: WILL THE FIGHTING EVER STOP?
YORKSHIRE'S BAD BLOOD RUNS EVERYWHERE

After being sacked, Boycs rang my dad, so overcome with sadness that he had to break off the conversation. 'I thought he might have been crying,' my dad said. Every player was asked whether Boycs ought to remain in the team. My dad unhesitatingly voted 'Yes'. Only two of his teammates did likewise. One of them was Arnie Sidebottom. My dad was part of the defence counsel for Boycs. He thought it 'made more sense to have him in the side'. He also thought: 'When he says Yorkshire cricket is his life, he is telling the truth.'

Boycs stayed at Yorkshire. At a special general meeting, which was like a high-noon showdown, his supporters won the vote to reinstate him. Boycs soon became a member of the general committee, and Brian Close was restored as chairman of the cricket sub-committee. You might find this hard to credit, since I'm describing events that occurred six years before I was born, but some of the feuds those rows cleaved open, as well as some of the wounds caused as a consequence of them, have still to heal. This isn't as plain daft as it sounds when you think of how heated the

exchanges between the opposing camps became. Or how a sense of proportion got lost amid the shouting. My dad suffered, implausibly called the 'head of the Yorkshire Mafia' and also the 'little bastard' responsible for 'causing all the trouble'. His accuser was a former Yorkshire committee member. In fact, my dad was a mediator, who loathed the infighting and remarked dryly of it: 'The trouble with revolutions is that anyone can be caught up in them.'

To be captain of Yorkshire was once described as being 'the second-best job on earth' – only half a notch below being captain of England. My dad had always wanted the job. As early as 1981 he confronted Illingworth about it at Scarborough. Illingworth had just made an uncapped player stand-in captain ahead of him. Exactly what was said depends on whose version you prefer. It was one of those yes-you-did and no-you-didn't sort of arguments, but the battle-lines between them were not under debate. My dad thought he should have been captain; Illingworth disagreed. What's also not in doubt is that my dad turned up the volume. Sailors in the Viking area of the North Sea are believed to have heard clearly what he said. Finally becoming captain in the summer of 1984, he was expected to bring together factions that were at loggerheads. No peacekeeper in the United Nations could have reconciled their differences. He was congratulated on his appointment by one member, who then warned him: 'Watch your back.'

My dad made two things clear. There should be 'no back-biting, no grudges', no traces of the ill will of Yorkshire's wintery discontent taken on to the field. He also didn't want to be a captain 'who led a team of losers'. These were optimistic ambitions, and he must have known it. He was constantly obliged to dodge a lot of criss-cross friendly fire, and every match was 'played in an atmosphere of crisis', he said.

On the morning of his first Championship match – against Somerset at Taunton – Boycs offered to give him a lift. He took a wrong turn and got lost. 'If Boycs didn't carry a map in his car, he wouldn't be able to find his way home,' my dad said. The two of them were late, but Yorkshire won in a run chase and went on an unbeaten streak lasting until the end of June. Injuries and a limited attack meant a 14th-place finish. The team also lost horrifically to Shropshire in the first round of the NatWest Trophy. His verdict was: 'We've been beaten by a team of amateurs, which doesn't say much for our professionals.'

My dad was unlucky. He always said he was less than a foot away from putting Yorkshire into the Benson & Hedges Cup final. In the semi, against Warwickshire at Headingley, he hit a shot, whistle-clean and out of the middle, but saw it taken on the boundary only because Bob Willis – 6 foot 6 tall in his bare feet – claimed the catch. Anyone else, lacking Willis's height and telescopic reach, would have watched the ball arc over them for a match-winning six. Being named man of the match was no consolation for my dad. 'Who remembers beaten semi-finalists?' he asked, mournfully. The defeat left a little cloud over him, and nothing could shift it for a while.

Captaincy was difficult for him at first. My dad found it hard to 'tell an old mate' that he wasn't in the team. He knew, too, that some saw him as a sergeant major, screaming orders, rather than an officer, pushing a fielder into position with a wave of his hand. Illingworth would later criticise him for that: 'People on the edge hear him shouting and yelling and they think he's a good skipper. But good captains don't do that.' When he took over, Yorkshire had attempted – but failed – to persuade him to hand the wicketkeeping gloves to someone else. Wicketkeeping was too important to give up, he said, but the difficulty of combining it and the captaincy was 'conveying the message'. As my dad said: 'You can't just wander up to a bowler and you can't always be running from where you are to them. Everything would take too long.' Anyway, he liked to lead Yorkshire the way he had always played for them, the noise he made integral to that.

My dad's time as captain was memorably described as 'a series of uphill cavalry charges'. The sentence is meant to illustrate not only Yorkshire's difficulty in grasping the initiative against teams that were more experienced and more heavily armed than them, but also the heart and guts and fight in my dad. I can think of a better analogy. His favourite film – which we watched so often as a family that we almost wore out first a video and then a DVD of it – was *Zulu*, which depicts the Battle of Rorke's Drift in 1879. Michael Caine had the breakthrough role of his career as Gonville Bromhead. My dad was more John Chard, the character played by Stanley Baker. *Zulu* is about how 150 soldiers held off three to four thousand warriors. Chard is told he hasn't got 'much of an army' at his disposal, but accepts it and makes a lot of very little. He continues to issue the same order – 'Front rank fire! Rear rank reload!' – to keep their spirit and momentum going, never slackening himself. Chard has most of the best lines in *Zulu*, and I can imagine my dad saying some of them. Told his troops are tired, he responds with: 'I don't give a damn – we fight on.' When Chard, just wounded, learns that Bromhead isn't overjoyed about having leadership responsibility shoved on to him, he says: 'You're a professional.'

Zulu was an inspirational film for my dad. He admired the red-coated British, but also admired the Zulus, who could run 50 miles towards the scene of a battle and still fight, fresh and fit, after getting there. Yorkshire was my dad's small army, outnumbered and outflanked but somehow surviving and occasionally prospering, if never coming too close to winning a trophy. He was always firing, always reloading, always aware that Yorkshire could be overrun at any moment. The subtleties of captaincy were less significant than the bloody-mindedness of just going on. It was a time of adjustment on the field and a typically unsettled one off it. Even Lord Hawke, dug up and dusted off, couldn't have done much better than my dad did.

It was still heretical to say then that Yorkshire ought to recruit from outside the county. My dad said it anyway, embroiled in a scrap over the recruitment of an overseas star. 'The game's changed,' he told the committee. 'You've got to fight fire with fire.' Yorkshire's loyalty to its own was a patriotically well-meaning but flawed act of intransigency. It persisted until 1992 when the county caved in, hiring at last a promising young fella you might have heard of: Sachin Tendulkar. On his arrival, he was immediately handed a flat cap and a pint of Tetley's so he could pose as an authentic Tyke for the newspaper photographers.

Odd how, 21 years later, I found myself standing at short leg to Tendulkar in a Test in Mumbai. I was crouched low and observing him through the grille of my helmet, amazed at the stillness of his body before the ball was bowled, the nimbleness of his feet as he picked the line and length of it, and also the depth of his bat, so thick that it seemed as though the whole trunk of a willow tree had been used to make it. Someone has only to mention Tendulkar and that image of him appears in front of me again, as though I am still there.

YORKSHIRE FINISHED 11TH in my dad's second season and 10th in his third, which was progression by inches. It wasn't enough for the committee, who wanted yards and so used the most unoriginal of excuses – that his wicketkeeping had 'suffered' because of his captaincy – to give the job to someone else. One of his favourite put-downs, delivered with gentle scepticism, was 'you know three-quarters of seven-eighths of sod all'. He believed it applied to Yorkshire then. He felt snubbed and also saw himself as a scapegoat. He recovered from that blow, returning to the ranks, but not subsequent ones. In 1988 he was dropped for the first time in his career. A year later the cricket committee decided to sack him, their decision reversed only after Brian Close's intervention. On a sunny day in June 1990 he *was* sacked, the news relayed in a phone call. That summer he'd ensured maximum batting points in one match and saved Yorkshire in two others. He was third in the club's Championship averages. 'I'm utterly devastated. I can't understand it,' he said. 'I will have to start counting my teeth because I've been kicked in the mouth so often.' He lost sleep about it too, admitting he'd once got up at 4 a.m. to check and recheck his run-scoring records and compare them with previous seasons.

I know my dad was reluctant to accept that Yorkshire were duty-bound to bed in a replacement for him eventually, and so he resented their efforts to do it. But the club were at fault too, refusing to placate him a little; for if you're constantly thrashed with a stick, rather than offered an olive branch, you're only going to respond one way. He asked a rhetorical question: 'How much does loyalty count?' It was meant to embarrass Yorkshire, a sign of how sour he felt towards them. Uncle Ted remembers how much his farewell disturbed him even 12 months later. He was still adamant about the unfairness of it. He was still certain that he ought to be playing. He was still talking about the principles of loyalty.

As far as the Championship was concerned, there was no sense of thwarted entitlement about it. He was simply aware that the team lacked the capacity to win the title while he was with them.

It was different for me.

WE NOT ONLY knew that we could win the Championship, but we also became quietly assured about it without ever feeling over-cocky. Before a ball was even bowled, there was a calm recognition that 2014 was 'our summer' – providing we put the work in.

We possessed what Yorkshire during my dad's day did not. We had a serious outbreak of talent. We had a set of bowlers who were capable of taking 20 wickets in a match. We had a set of batsmen who were capable of scoring a thousand-plus runs or at least coming close to it. We also had a squad with depth to it. We recruited well from overseas – first Kane Williamson, then Aaron Finch – but we also had lots of good pros who were on the edge of our team and could have muscled into quite a few others (19 different names appeared in our scorebook).

This isn't an infallible rule, but I look at successful Championship sides and mostly see in them a collection of players who fit into one of three categories. Those who performed with distinction for England in the recent past, but either know another call is unlikely to come or have retired internationally anyway. I'm thinking of Ryan Sidebottom. Those who have already played in a few Test matches, been dropped and want more than anything to reclaim a place. Someone like me, for instance. And those who are hungry for a first Test cap and go out to get one, such as Adam Lyth, Gary Ballance and Adil Rashid.

Even then, during the long haul of the summer, you can only cross your fingers about the two factors no one has control over. The weather, especially in the blowy north, has to be kind. And usually – for this was before the introduction of the uncontested toss – the coin has to spin and fall the right way for you. It didn't for us. We guessed right only five times, which statistically proves that Lady Luck didn't love us as tenderly as she might have done. The fact that we still blasted other counties apart tells you the fighting shape we were in. Partly it was because of our ravenous desire for success; Yorkshire had won only that one title in 46 years. More significantly we knew the sweat we'd have to shed to achieve it, making us psychologically stronger than ever before.

In 2013 the club celebrated its 150th anniversary. There was a lot of hoopla around our sesquicentennial: dinners, books, commemorative souvenirs, a smart striped blazer tailored in the club's colours to exactly match one that Lord Hawke once wore. We were among the bookmakers' Championship favourites, adding to the pressure and expectation that gathered around our attempt to crown the celebratory year. In many seasons winning seven matches would have been enough for us to do it. Not then. We came second to Durham, losing to them in one of those epic contests in Scarborough during the festival. Defeat wiped away the decent lead we then held and also gave them the impetus to cash in on a game in hand. We didn't complain, acknowledging Durham as the marginally superior team. But being so close brought us a wider appreciation than before of what would be needed to push us over the line next time.

The modern cricketer has access to a heap of data. Every season is scrupulously logged. It's like an annual census of your career. Not only statistically, in the form of coloured charts, tables and diagrams, but also in video. You can get a recording of every innings you play, rewatching them on a laptop until your eyes pop and your mind frazzles. But we stripped everything down to the basics. Nothing about our strategy was ever too fussy or over-elaborate. Andrew Gale, our captain, spoke the phrase 'process, process, process' so often that he probably said it aloud in his sleep. It only meant repeating the next day what we'd done successfully during the previous one, each of us fulfilling our own responsibilities.

We took the title emphatically and aggressively, unquestionably the best and the most attractive side. Five games were won by an innings. We romped through another by almost 300 runs, a second by more than 200 and a third by nine wickets. At Northampton our openers Adam Lyth and Alex Lees piled up an opening partnership of 375 and made almost 2,500 runs between them throughout the summer, bossing the Championship the way Justin Langer and Matthew Hayden had once bossed Tests for Australia. The bowling wasn't only bullied; it was flayed and tanned too. Here's the maths that matter: nine batsmen – and I was one of them – averaged over 40 and six bowlers averaged below 30. We dominated even those games we drew. We lost only once – at Lord's in late April. Middlesex chased down a fantasy score of nearly 500, a defeat that would have subsequently ripped the backbone and the bleeding heart out of weaker teams. You have nightmares but forget them when you next turn out the light for bed. This is one that happened to us in broad daylight and while we were awake, but we treated the experience as you should any bad dream, forgetting it and moving on. We proved unstoppable because of that. We stampeded through August and into September, our results carrying us to Trent Bridge for the penultimate game against Notts, who were then in second place. If we could beat them, the Championship was ours.

It was one of those games in which the sun shone strongly, making it seem as though high summer was still to come. The law of averages kicked in too. We won the toss, a rarity. We totted up over 500 runs, making them in no hurry. We pinned Notts to the floor and held them there.

Jack Brooks rattled off 68 wickets in the season, mostly from short, rat-a-tat spells. We used him in spurts rather like the Australians had deployed Mitchell Johnson during the Ashes series. Trent Bridge, however, was Ryan Sidebottom's stage. My dad's on-field relationship with Tony Nicholson in the 1970s became symbiotic – almost telepathic, even. It wasn't only that my dad could tell, simply from the way Nicholson spread his fingers on the seam, whether he planned to swing the ball away, bring it back or make it shoot upwards off a length. He could also detect from Nicholson's body language – how tall he stood, the angle of his shoulders, the stride of his walk – how he was feeling at a particular hour, which meant he read, as easily as words on a page, how his friend would bowl. It's the same for me with Sid. I can see when he's about to take the opposition out. He'll throw back that thick tangle of hair. He'll stick his chest and his chin out a little further. He'll look at a batsman as though mentally boring a hole straight through him.

The chance he was being offered seemed too perfectly coincidental to be true. Here he found himself, back at the club that had curiously let him go, with the ball in his hand and the glint of the Championship ahead of him. Dear me; Notts were about to pay. In the first innings he took three for 35. In the second, as Notts followed on, I've never seen him bowl better. He blazed away at them. He made the ball do everything except come back into his hand after leaving it like a yo-yo. It was a classical demonstration of seam and swing and accuracy, a piece of cricketing art. The MCC could have produced an instructional DVD purely from one spell. In 18.2 overs he claimed six for 30.

At 11.36 a.m. on the final morning, beneath a clear sky, one of my mates was bowling to another: it was Sid versus James Taylor. Titch slog-slashed a slightly short and wide ball to backward point. Game over. Championship won.

My dad once said that if he ever won a trophy for Yorkshire he'd cry his eyes out. He did it twice. I don't mind admitting that I wept at Trent Bridge too, as the consequence of our achievement sank in. So did Sid. We'd come so far together and scrambled over so many hurdles to get there. A lot of what we felt went unspoken only because each of us knew what was going through the other's mind, our past experiences and our expression making words unnecessary. We were thinking about my dad ... and about his dad ... about how much we owed our respective families, who were there ... about him proving Notts wrong at last ... about my fight to get over Australia and get back into the England team ... about Yorkshire being at the top again ... about how proud we felt.

It was one of those days that will stay with me always, however old I grow. I won't forget the sound of 'On Ilkley Moor Baht 'At', a burst of community singing that rose from nowhere. Or the endless bottles of Veuve Clicquot sprayed across the outfield, which surely grew lusher over the winter because so much of the champagne got soaked into the grass. Or how, not far from the square, Sid and I played football with his children, Darley and Indiana, the shadows getting longer as the afternoon wore slowly on. Or the fact that none of us really wanted to go home, doing so only reluctantly, like moving a party elsewhere, when the ground was empty and the light was dropping. There is no time like the first time. I looked around me, savouring what I saw and storing images as memories, adding to those that I'd snapped with my mobile phone.

A few months later Yorkshire fastened a team picture on to the wall near our dressing rooms. It remains there now.

In the photograph, taken at Headingley after the season's last match, we're behind the obligatory sponsors' board. Each of us has an arm raised in triumph. The Lord's Taverners chalice is raised too. Whenever I pass it, the picture reminds me of our achievement and also of the whole spread of that super summer. But the most poignant thing isn't the image on its own, but the place where Yorkshire chose to put it. It sits directly below another photograph – the one of my dad on the Lord's balcony after the Benson & Hedges Cup final.

So there we are, dad and son alongside one another again, celebrating triumphs that are 27 years apart.

THAT TITLE-WINNING SEASON turned my career right-side up again. It made possible all that followed immediately afterwards.

I was behind the stumps for 12 successive first-class matches, which counts as my longest-ever run for Yorkshire. I settled into a groove, the simple familiarity with routine and repetition improving me as a wicketkeeper. I felt more confident purely because I'd taken more deliveries. I regained my form and my zeal for the game. I became a different player.

Nine members of the Yorkshire team at Trent Bridge had come through the academy, so retaining the Championship in 2015 was hardly unexpected. We won more matches (11) than any side since the split into two divisions. We racked up more points (286) than anyone had done over that same period. And our margin of victory (68 points) was the most convincing too. From the start of that season until the late middle of it in particular, the runs came in a lovely long flood for me. I'd finish with a Championship average of 92.33. In May there was a hundred against Hampshire. In June there was another century against Middlesex and then a career-best double hundred – 219 not out at Durham. Barely a week afterwards, as July began, I went to Warwickshire, scoring 108, and then to Worcestershire, adding another 139.

The Ashes series had been going on without me. We'd beaten Australia at Cardiff. They'd beaten us – rather badly – at Lord's. I'd been on the England Lions tour of South

Africa the previous winter. As though history were repeating itself, purely for my benefit, I'd also been called up for the last ODI of the series against New Zealand at Chester-le-Street in June when Jos Buttler split the webbing in his hand. Like my first ODI at Cardiff four years previously, the game was rain-affected. This wasn't the only spooky similarity. The matches were almost mirror images of one another. We again found ourselves chasing a total that Duckworth–Lewis set. I went in – again – when things seemed fruitless for us; we were 40 for four. And I won man of the match too: 83 off 60 balls led us to a win with an over to spare. Eighteen months had still rushed by since I'd last appeared in a Test before sheer weight of runs – almost a thousand at 80-something – got me back for the third Test at Edgbaston. Some things had changed. England were under new management. Trevor Bayliss had replaced Peter Moores, sacked after only 13 months. Some things hadn't changed at all.

Mitchell Johnson was waiting for me.

On pitches that didn't offer as much bounce, muzzling him a bit, Johnson hadn't been as successful here as he'd been on the hard soil of home. This isn't to say he was docile. I'd made five when I faced my first ball from him on the second morning of the match. Johnson, who beforehand had barely got a delivery much above stomach height, thrust one in short of a length. The ball rose, screaming blue murder. I edged it in front of my face and Peter Nevill, Australia's wicketkeeper, took it in front of his. Even Geoffrey Boycott, seldom short of something pithy to say, initially offered only three words. These were 'what a delivery', and the astonished tone of his voice suggested that a platoon of exclamation marks were trailing behind the short sentence. The term 'rip-snorter' came later. So did the follow-up description 'an absolutely lethal ball'.

Anyone looking at the scorecard could conclude that Johnson had a spell over me; that he simply had to turn his arm over to get me out. Not so. The delivery was a jaffa, a beast for any right-handed batsman. Even watching the replay three-dozen times wouldn't have given me much of a clue about how I could have played it and been certain of survival. Two balls later a similar, but not quite as spiteful, delivery from Johnson got rid of Ben Stokes.

The main thing was that we won the Test and then took the next at Trent Bridge, where I got 74. We regained there what we'd lost in Australia, which was the grandest form of redemption after our previous trouncing. I finished the season with more than 1,100 runs, a second Ashes-winning medal and a second County Championship. And only three and a half months later, I was at the crease in Cape Town on 99 not out, waiting for Stiaan van Zyl to finally drop a delivery a little short and wide of off stump …

Stokesy and I had a partnership with bells and whistles attached to it that day. We trampled across the record books, revising them as we went. His double hundred was the second fastest in Test history. The 399 we put on together was a world record for the sixth wicket – and the first 300 of them constituted the fastest triple-hundred stand in Tests.

You'd become figure-blind if I listed the other landmarks that got overtaken. In the end I made 150 not out, the last half-century coming off 30 balls – all the tension purged at last. You'd think Newlands was the launch pad for the unprecedented 12 months that followed, bringing more hundreds and more record breaking.

It wasn't.

It actually began in a restaurant beside the Indian Ocean.

CHAPTER 10

A DAMP DAY IN FRONT OF THE WESTERN TERRACE

I KNOW EVERYONE draws first the easy straight line that connects me to my dad. I don't blame them, but in doing so one fact, which is the most important of all, usually goes unnoticed or gets ignored. I look so much like my dad – same chin, same cheekbones, same forehead – and I play a little like him too. But I am my mother's son. I am who I am because of her. My dad passed on his cricketing talent. My mum has enabled me to use it. Her life's work has been Becky and me. She's given our lives balance and structure. She's taught us to treat everyone decently and equally. Our sense of spirit and our guts come from her. So does our work ethic.

Without my dad, she had to be fatherly as well as motherly. As we broke into our teens, she could never rely on that 'wait till your father gets home' approach. She had to pull us into line herself, responsible for all the dos and don'ts and also any tellings-off. In having to be tough, she worried that she wasn't being tender enough at the same time and that what we'd remember of our childhood were only the rebukes she'd given us rather than the love. Never. We remember only the love.

I knew my mum was giving – and would always give – everything she could and more to Becky and me. The money she had went on us. The time she had was ours. I knew, though she never spoke about it, how isolated she must have felt sometimes, bringing up the two of us practically alone. Her investment in us came at an enormous personal cost. Her diary and her social life became entirely dominated by our own. As children do, we must have infuriated and exasperated her, no doubt in the same moment. We only wanted her to be happy, but some days we must have been more of a benign nuisance than a help. There must have been other days, too, when she was fed up or despondent, but she didn't betray it to us, going on indomitably instead and thinking of us first and herself hardly at all.

She didn't even complain about her cancer. I've never heard her ask 'why me?' – though the question would not only be legitimate but also perfectly understandable for someone who has been through so much so often. My mum thinks I get my determination and resilience from my dad. I think it comes mostly from her. She's recovered from each setback and every adversity, demonstrating a resilience that constantly astonishes me.

Like my dad's death, Becky and I recall my mum's original diagnosis of cancer and then her treatment in fragments. Most of all, we remember how tired she became and how long it took for her to get well again. Also like my dad's death, she explained her cancer to us – or as much as she dared – without ever getting emotional, aware as ever of our feelings.

Everyone who survives cancer knows the victory against it may only be temporary. You know eventually that you might have to fight all over again. Almost 15 years after my mum's first bout of cancer, a second bout occurred. This time she needed an operation.

It was the winter of 2012, only four days before Christmas. I was on England's tour of India. My mum didn't want me to know what was happening to her in case it affected my form. She decided that I shouldn't be told until after the surgeon had done his work. Only Becky changed her mind. 'You've got to tell him,' she said. 'He'll want to come home and be with you.' Becky continued to press that point. The way she felt was the way I would feel, she argued. 'I'd be heartbroken if I learnt about the operation only after it was over.'

I was in Pune, a city that is one of the symbols of the new, vibrant India. The temperature was over 30 degrees. Your mobile phone is locked away when a game starts, so England's security officer Reg Dickason had to bring me a message. It was no more than a solemn 'your mum wants to speak to you', a handful of words that I knew were drenched in meaning. It couldn't be anything but bad news. I was on the outfield, preparing for the match. I ran off to reclaim my phone, saying nothing to anyone at first. I called my mum without being able to reach her, the phone useless in my hand. 'I need to know what's wrong,' I said to Reg.

So he told me.

The trek home began as a long day's journey into a sleepless night. Mumbai is only 90 miles away from Pune, but the drive there took five hours. The wait for a flight to Manchester took five hours more. The flight itself took 12 hours. I touched down at 10 a.m. I was on the road almost an hour later. Since it was the weekend before Christmas, the holiday rush had already begun, the traffic so thick as one motorway merged into another that it took almost two hours to travel from the airport to the hospital in York. The car got stuck in a jam and I told the driver in panic: 'Please, just get me there somehow ... any how ... any way.' I arrived just 20 minutes before my mum was wheeled into theatre for an 11-hour operation. There was just enough time to kiss her and hold her hand. The ward had been spruced up with tinsel and posted-up cards in an attempt to make it look festive. I didn't notice them.

The hospital released my mum so she could spend Christmas at home with us. I helped cook dinner – though none too skilfully on my part – with Becky. We fetched and carried and fussed over her, the fact that she was there and recovering more important than presents or food or decorations.

Exactly three years later the three of us were in very different surroundings, which made it especially poignant. The Oyster Box hotel in Durban sits on the Umhlanga seaside. The beach is decorated by an 80-foot lighthouse, the crown of it redder than my hair, that sits on the Indian Ocean, which stretches like a blue carpet to the horizon. The

Oyster Box is a five-star palace, and Becky and I took Mum to the restaurant there, an early 60th-birthday present for her. The perfect day is one in which nothing can be added afterwards to make it even better in the memory. We had that perfect day. Becky, I know, counts it as 'one of the happiest' we've ever spent together. We wanted to be nowhere else in the world then – and in no one else's company except our own. The sun was full. The sky and the sea were empty, each attempting to outdo the other for bright colour. The afternoon was still and meandered on beautifully and we took our time to enjoy it, enticing Mum to eat mussels and scallops, which usually she wouldn't, and also taste drinks she hadn't sampled before. Mostly we

talked … and we talked … and then we talked some more. Our mum was healthy and fit; only that mattered to us.

The series against South Africa began at Kingsmead on Boxing Day. I walked into it with my head and my game together, the thought of our perfect day relaxing me. I made one half-century and came close to another. We won the Test by a landslide of runs. The Oyster Box had put me in the mood for Durban. And then Durban put me in the mood for Cape Town. We went on to beat South Africa 2–1, losing only the dead rubber, and I reached a turning point with England, a place where my century had carried me. But to push on and take advantage of it, I knew one thing had to improve.

If it didn't, I'd be dropped.

AT THE STAGE at which I seriously started to think about becoming a wicketkeeper, Adam Gilchrist was in his pomp. Everybody wanted to be like him.

It can be difficult to judge the scale of something when you're actually living through it, but Gilchrist was recognised as a game-changer while he was still playing rather than only retrospectively. He was one of those once-in-a-generation cricketers, the batsman-wicketkeeper par excellence. What impressed me, then as well as now, was how he did that: how he broke down the component parts of the two roles, working out an approach that suited him, and then how his work ethic shot him to the top. I liked the fact that he set out to dominate the bowling aggressively, irrespective of who had the ball and how the field was set. He argued – correctly – that the game was about 'hitting in the ball'. He could smash it anywhere, but was especially strong off the back foot, his pulls as vicious as a boxer's haymaker to the jaw. I also liked the fact that everything – as well as keeping wicket – was done without fuss.

Nothing excellent is ever wrought suddenly. Gilchrist is proof of that, but he's also proof of what careful thought, allied to application and the shedding of several hundred gallons of sweat, can achieve. After all, here was someone originally viewed as a batter who 'kept a bit'. Here was someone forced to swap New South Wales for Western Australia because he wasn't rated as the best in his own state. And here was someone who eloquently expressed how he felt when chosen only as a batsman. Gilchrist frequently fielded close in or as a short-something or other for New South Wales, but regarded not wearing the gloves and pads as being 'almost naked'. Without them, he added, he was 'only half a cricketer'. Gilchrist thought not being the wicket-keeper applied more pressure on his batting, which made him jittery. If he failed, he feared being 'out altogether' and soon forgotten.

What he underwent at Western Australia was nothing short of a metamorphosis, and it led to the reinvention of the wicketkeeper-batsman for the modern era. He remod-elled the strategy of that role the way the aeroplane and aerial bombardment once remodelled the strategy of war. In 2001 Duncan Fletcher, then the England coach, put together a tactics book for the Ashes, detailing the strengths and weaknesses of the Australians. Against Gilchrist's name, he wrote a question mark. His strengths were too numerable and his weaknesses too debatable. The question mark was the equivalent of a baffled Fletcher scratching his head about him.

My dad and I aren't the only Bairstows to have played for Yorkshire as a wicketkeeper. Arthur Bairstow was another Bradfordian, which isn't surprising since the surname has its Anglo-Saxon origins in West Yorkshire. He was even born in the same block of the city as my dad, but, as far as I'm aware, he's no relation unless he lurks on the outer fringes of our family tree. You probably won't have heard of him unless you've delved into the minutiae of the county's history. That's because his brief moment in the sun came between the fag end of the Victorian era and the start of the Edwardian one. He didn't do that badly. In 26 matches he took 41 catches and 18 stumpings. His batting, however, was lamentable. He made only 79 runs. His highest score was 12. His average was 5.64. It's hard to believe that wicket-keepers haven't always been expected to contribute runs, but were considered as specialists. Gilchrist put an end to that way of thinking for ever. Now, if you can't bat you don't play.

Wicketkeepers will perish without them, but big scores alone are no protection if catches go down and stumpings go begging. Gilchrist knew that too. My dad used to say that 'a catch is either held or it goes in the blink of an eye'. Some had gone in the blink of an eye for me in South Africa. In the first Test I'd missed a chance off Hashim Amla (cost six runs). In the fourth Test I'd missed him again (cost 104 runs). And a difficult stumping to get rid of AB de Villiers escaped me in Durban (cost 34 runs). The nine catches I took in Johannesburg didn't attract as much attention as those mistakes.

Every slip will nag at you; that's the consequence of being human. The hardest thing – and it's entirely psychological – is not allowing an error to spread into the rest of your game and multiply, infecting the whole of it like a virus. You have to shut it away, start again and stay composed, not only at the time but also afterwards when you can see the post-match criticism coming towards you as visible as tracers. I used to read newspapers. I used to follow social media, drawn by curiosity to know what others were saying and thinking about me. I discovered that that way madness lies.

Something soon dawned on me, possibly too slowly but only because I was much younger then, less worldly wise and the pitfalls weren't as well-defined. I learnt that when you get into the public eye, assumptions are made about you; especially about the sort person you are and the kind of personality you have – as though watching someone on TV stacks up enough evidence to form an indisputable judgement about them. I also learnt that 99 per cent of those assumptions are wrong. Some of them bizarrely so. I've been called a disgrace to my family, a disgrace to my country, a disgrace to myself. Upsetting at first, it now bounces off me like rain off a roof.

I stopped listening to professional critics as well. Bob Willis once likened me to a seal on a rock, floundering and flapping for the ball. Probably Willis doesn't get enough credit for 1981 and the 500–1 Miracle of Headingley. Ian Botham's nuclear blast with the bat meant the Test will always carry his stamp of ownership, his runs overshadowing Willis's wickets. With his mop of hair and jerky run made on stick-like limbs, Willis polished Australia off with eight for 43 in the second innings, a stint of bowling that at any other time and in any other circumstances would have brought him the laurels and the lap of the honour. Even if he'd never achieved this, his fast-bowling career would still count as superb. My dad certainly thought so. But I don't know how often – if at all – Willis has ever kept wicket. So

I listen instead to other wicketkeepers, such as Mark Boucher, who I sought out in South Africa. Or MS Dhoni, who I saw during a tour of India. Or Matt Prior, helpful whenever I played alongside him.

You can ask and ask, collating as much advice as you can carry, but in the end you still have to find your own way, your own style and your own method. Just as Gilchrist did. What you need is a coach who understands that. Someone who shares their expertise without imposing it on you inflexibly. Someone who understands that coaching should be bespoke and not off the peg. Someone who allows you to develop naturally, so you find out things for yourself. Someone who won't soft-soap you. And especially someone you can trust.

Step forward Bruce French, minus his boa constrictor.

IT WAS A bitter, depressing March morning, the bruised cloud so low that you felt it could hardly sink much lower without smothering the whole of Headingley like the thickest of pea-soup fogs. It was damp, which made the grass soft and skiddy, and so cold that you'd have thought the hollow of winter was still with us. The Oyster Box in Durban and my century in Cape Town seemed to belong to another year – even another decade – rather than only a month and a half past.

In the conditions – we even got some sleety snow later on – only the slightly insane would have headed anywhere except indoors. But I knew I needed to sharpen up my wicket-keeping, which meant I also needed Bruce French. The work we had to do required space and fresh air. That's why we found ourselves in such miserably awful weather in front of the Western Terrace, the dark-blue rows of seats where, during a Test, it is almost obligatory to come in fancy dress.

There wasn't a soul about. If anyone glimpsed us, it was from behind glass. Frenchy and I had the run of the place to ourselves – at least once I'd sweet-talked Yorkshire's groundsman Andy Fogarty into letting us train there. After months of work, the new season almost on top of him, he wasn't too enamoured by the prospect of the two of us tearing chunks out of his turf. Like a good golfer, we promised to flatten any divots afterwards; he made sure we did, too.

Brian Statham, new-ball partner and chum of Fred Trueman, once described his preparation for a game like this: 'A fag, a cough, a cup of coffee.' He was talking essentially about the 1950s. Even during my dad's era – certainly at the beginning of it – practice still wasn't overly sophisticated or particularly strenuous either. The calendar was such a treadmill of matches and travelling that you barely had a day or two between one and the next. You kept fit and in decent nick simply through playing. Now we stretch or catch, pummel the ball into a net or throw down a single stump. But the real graft, the hardest shift, is put in when there's no one there to watch it.

It was Frenchy's recommendation to Andy Flower that led to my one-day international debut at Cardiff. I'd been taking his advice ever since I began moving from one staging post to the next with England. Frenchy likes climbing. It's no weekend pursuit or casual hobby for him either. He's been in the Himalayas. He's scaled the Scottish sea stacks. At Headingley, he was dressed as though he was about to go up Annapurna. I was swathed in clothes too – but still freezing.

He's a hard taskmaster. There's no mucking about; Frenchy isn't slow or shy about letting you know when something is wrong. I needed his clear eye and his straight talking.

I don't like intensely complicated coaching. I prefer to work things out by myself. A gentle hint is all I need; otherwise it's like finishing a crossword after someone has given me the answers, some of which may not be right anyway. I don't go in for coaching manuals either. I always ask: Who wrote them? More often than not it's someone who isn't a Test cricketer – or it's someone who was, but hasn't played in a Test since Margaret Thatcher was Prime Minister. Ian Dews knows I'm not into too much 'technical crap'. He also knows I don't respond to being told explicitly what to do. He'll simply say to me: 'This is what I'm seeing,' allowing me to work out what I need to do.

Yorkshire once had the foresight to take on the sports psychologist David Priestley, another Bradford lad. He was subsequently attached first to Saracens rugby club and then to Arsenal football club, endorsing his pedigree. Early on in my career, when my mental approach to batting had become rather confused, I went to him to talk about sorting it out. I don't think our conversation lasted much longer than ten minutes. We sat opposite one another at a table. He handed over a blank sheet of paper and a pen, asking me to outline what I believed were the basic principles of my game. I'm paring to the bone what I said, but essentially I told him:

See the ball
Hit the ball
Dominate
Keep it simple

He didn't say anything as I spoke or when I wrote them down, shortening my sentences to turn them into bullet points. I slid the piece of paper towards him. He read it and then slid the paper back to me again. 'This is your blueprint,' he said. 'Use it.' You might regard that as money for several yards of old rope, but he saw instantly what I couldn't and he then enabled me to see it too, as though a lens had been tweaked, bringing everything into focus. In reflecting my own thoughts back to me he also put them in perspective, untangling the problem. I'd been overthinking things. I had that piece of paper laminated. I took it around with me as a prompter, always there alongside my kit.

My approach to wicketkeeping is a minor variation of my approach to batting. I see the ball; I catch the ball. Though only those who don't do the job still think of it as being that simple. In South Africa, for example, I'd been standing just a little wide, the weight transferring too heavily on to my left foot. I had to adjust. I've gradually changed my technique as challenges to it have cropped up, always making calibrated adjustments to manage them. For a while I used the half-squat, which has become known as the power position. Then I went back to the old-school full-squat. I became less static, developing more movement in the way I kept too.

At Headingley, I wanted Frenchy to go through the mechanics of everything with me again in the same way that Ian would look at my batting.

Frenchy dragged out what looks like a bowling machine set up at floor-level. The ball comes out of it at anywhere from 50 to 55 miles per hour. He stood in front of me with a miniature bat, making it harder to guess whether the delivery would come straight through or take a snick. He'd later hurl a ball into a ridged, sloping board, which would send me diving everywhere – high, low, at full-length sideways and upwards, like someone possessed. There was also a session with the slip cradle, the design of which hasn't fundamentally changed since its invention before the last war. Frenchy slung balls into it and I stood at close range. He peppered me with catches that came very fast and very hard.

I've been through practices during which I've felt as though medieval torture would have been easier to handle. Once, in India, the day was hot enough to melt metal. If I made a mistake, I had to take off all my kit – gloves, inners, pads, box – and then put them all back on again, beginning from scratch. I hated it.

Nothing nonetheless was more arduous than my day with Frenchy. I got angry and frustrated with myself, with the drills, with everything. I was catching balls on my left hip … my right hip … with a single hand … with both hands. I was thinking about my natural foot movement … the dives I had to make … holding on to the ball as my elbow jarred against the grass. The lonely sound of the ball against the cradle, off the board or from the bat and into my gloves echoed around the ground. The other noise came from the strangled shouts I made whenever I dropped or couldn't get near a catch. At the end my palms throbbed, my fingers stung. I was soaked to the skin too.

When I came into the England team I was always being asked to the point of tedium whether I 'really' wanted to be a wicketkeeper as well as a batsman. It was as though no one had noticed or taken seriously the work I'd already put in to make myself one. I got tetchy about it, sometimes barely suppressing my incredulity that anyone would think I didn't want the gloves. On that filthy day, the practice over at last, I walked towards our dressing rooms – wet, exhausted, achy – wishing that anyone who had ever put the question to me could have been there and seen every second of the previous three hours. Only a masochist – or someone who wanted to be a wicketkeeper very much – would have pushed themselves that hard.

THE NUMBER OF Test runs I scored during 2016 eclipses in the public mind the number of dismissals I claimed because catches and stumpings will always be less glamorous than hundreds. You rarely get a headline for taking a leg-side edge or two – only for dropping one. But I know every successful day I had in the field could be traced back to that session with Bruce French.

Wicketkeeping is an extreme physical and mental challenge. In 12 months, during 17 Tests played in locations as diverse as Manchester and Visakhapatnam, I did more than 17,000 squats. I encountered some pitches where the ball came into my gloves with a hammer-like thump and others where I had to take it in front of my shins. Sometimes the variation in a bowler's wrist position is minimal but critical; even Jimmy Anderson doesn't always know what a delivery will do when it leaves his hand. So I, like the batsman, have a split second to decide where to go, calculating line, length and speed, doing so sometimes when the flight path of the ball is partly obscured. One of more than half-a-dozen things can happen to it in the air or off the pitch. Preparing yourself for each of them is a constant battle.

Frenchy designed our work to cope with that. My confidence improved. So did my concentration. Against Bangladesh in Chittagong, where the temperature was up towards the mid-30s, the ball turned prodigiously on a dusty pitch that was as hard as a stone-slabbed floor. Each innings was a long examination of patience, endurance, hand–eye coordination and the fundamental skills of standing up to the wicket. I passed it, thanks to that miserably damp day at Headingley. And because I felt better about my wicketkeeping, I also felt better about my batting – and vice versa.

My dad was superstitious to a slavish degree that he called 'ridiculous'. Everything had to be done as a trinity. He'd pat the ground three times. He'd slam his bat into the block hole three times. He'd fiddle at his gloves three times. For a while he carried a lucky medallion, which a stranger had given him in a pub. I'm not usually like that, but I confess I was reluctant to change either my gloves or my inners, however tattered the fabric became, in case somehow it interrupted the streak I was on.

Once, after stumping Mike Brearley at Lord's, my dad admitted that he didn't know how the ball had ended up in his hands, asking himself afterwards: 'What on earth am I doing here?' He was in the zone, the state in which you're so absorbed in what you're doing that everything comes so automatically and you can't explain it. You're barely conscious of what you're accomplishing. You're not always aware of your surroundings.

That summer, and then the winter that followed it, became a bit like that for me.

Somehow cricketers – perhaps the statistical element of the game encourages it – tend to have the savant's remarkable recall for dates and detail, able to bring back in a snap how a wicket fell or how a shot went to the boundary. The weather, the condition of the pitch and sometimes even the position of the field comes back to us also. My mum will tell you about the interminable conversations she sat through, often under extreme sufferance, as my dad and his team-mates went over games as though they'd been played last weekend rather than a decade or two before. My dad kept a bag of old cricket balls, each of them worn to varying degrees. He labelled none of them, but knew which belonged to what match simply from looking at the scuff marks. He could then go through the match without the need of the scorecard.

I've got the same power of recall. In 2016, from Cape Town to Chennai, I can remember almost every notable ball I took or faced in every match. I always will.

By the end of it I'd made 1,470 runs – more than any wicketkeeper in a calendar year, beating Andy Flower's 1,045. I'd chalked up three centuries and eight half-centuries. I'd come within 12 of overtaking Michael Vaughan, whose 1,481 runs in 2002 are the most scored by an England batsman in a calendar year. I'd taken 70 dismissals – 66 catches and four stumpings – to establish another record.

Most of the records I set during the year were on top of me and then over before I realised it. The advance publicity for my pursuit of Vaughan's total, however, was inescapable. I knew, going into that last innings, that I needed only a modest score to overtake him. Afterwards I couldn't believe that I'd been idiotic enough to send a leg-side half-volley towards Ravindra Jadeja, who is India's best fielder. Nor could I believe that in the first innings, with another fifty there for the taking, I'd chipped a catch to extra cover when I'd intended simply to push for a single. I regret missing that record so much. Records are important even though you know that someone will come along and break them eventually. They're like the hallmark on a piece of gold or silver, telling everyone the worth of it. Records aren't subjective either. No one can dispute them the way opinions are disputed. And for as long as your name sits alongside one, you'll be able to point to it – even when you've gone grey – offering proof of the sort of player you were.

'Question marks gave way to exclamation marks,' was *Wisden*'s generous appraisal of those performances, also referring to my 'ingrained desire to prove critics wrong'.

I started it, appropriately enough, on home soil.

It's odd to admit, at least for someone as young as I am, but I have a 'bucket list', and the first item on it used to be: score a Test century at Headingley. The old ground doesn't get as many Test matches as it once did – I'd played in only one before, against New Zealand, and got into the 60s – so the chance for a hundred would have to be taken when it was there because I couldn't be sure when, or if, I'd get another.

We were 83 for five against Sri Lanka on another of those mornings that wouldn't have made the cover of the Visit Yorkshire tourist brochure. It was overcast, the light dim. Alastair Cook thought afterwards that I'd taken my own pitch out with me and rolled it across the square because, he said, I 'played so differently from anyone else'. Despite our dire position, I wanted to be aggressive without being reckless. I like to fight in a corner rather than cower in it.

In a Twenty20 match for Yorkshire, played early on in my career, about 30 university mates came to watch me from the Western Terrace. I was sent to the mid-wicket boundary, directly in front of them. Lo and behold, I soon got an absolute skier of a catch, one of those that seems to hover in hot air, like a bird searching for prey, and takes five minutes to fall. I got under the ball, cupping my hands and planting my feet firmly in textbook fashion to take it. Then I dropped the bloody thing. There was a horrid, almost eerie silence before my mates began to cheer loudly, aware that there was no point in pretending the small disaster hadn't happened. It counts as my most embarrassing moment in cricket.

Some of my closest friends – seven of them to be exact – surprised me at the Test. I'd donated one of my old England shirts to each of them, which meant a few rugby players, who usually wore XXXL, forced their amply shaped frames into something at least three sizes too small for them. But I didn't know, until the match started, that those shirts would be supplemented by ginger wigs and masks. The masks were a photograph of my face with the eyes scissored out. This group of friends, like the previous lot, were tucked near the back of the Western Terrace. I started to plug away for them. I got into the 30s briskly, reached a half-century and then moved gradually from one stage to the next – into the 60s, through the 70s and beyond the 80s. I came within sight of my hundred, so close that the luckiest of inside edges could have been enough, when we lost two quick wickets. I imagined myself stranded on 98.

Steven Finn came in at number ten. He's known as the Watford Wall, a name that reflects a resolute 'thou shall not pass' resistance from him. He may not make many runs, but in his hands the bat is a formidably wide barrier. 'Don't worry. We'll get you there,' he said. The Wall is always eager to go for a run. At the start of the 78th over, I drove Dushmantha Chameera to short extra cover. The Wall, sensing a chance, was off almost before I hit it. His sprint flustered the fielder, who was enticed into making a rash throw towards the non-striker's end. The ball whistled past the stumps and ended up deep into the outfield because no one had been able to back up. We scampered two runs, and

suddenly my bucket list had one fewer thing on it. I liked the 'well done' without words that Jack Brooks promptly posted on Twitter. It was a picture of a ginger snap.

I learnt during the Sri Lanka series how far I'd come in four years. I compared the 22-year-old who'd made his debut at Lord's with the 26-year-old who went back there only three weeks after Headingley. Everything about me was different. Stance. Body language. Approach. Attitude. My bucket list was different too. At the top now was: score a Test century at Lord's.

We had been coasting on 50-odd without loss. By the time I went in, we'd sunk inexplicably to 84 for four. Nothing unsettled me. Not our parlous position. Not being dropped early on at mid-wicket. Not an lbw shout so perilous that I survived it only by the width of a hair. I'll never forget one shot when the end of the first day was looming. It was a steer off my legs: a half-step back, a simple nudge into the lengthening shadows behind square. I watched the ball as it rolled into the wide gap towards the edge of the Grandstand, giving me one of the easiest singles of my career. I set off for it, knowing I'd have a hundred once I got to the other end. I could almost jog there rather than rush, allowing me just enough time to savour properly some of the scenes unfolding around me: the crowd standing as one in salute, the raised hands and the raised voices, my teammates clustered together behind the white railings of the balcony.

Sky Sports filmed the moment when my name went on to the honours board. It was humbling to think this merest sliver of the place would always be mine, and more humbling still to contemplate that I'd achieved something that much more illustrious names never had, among them Brian Lara, Ricky Ponting, Sunil Gavaskar and even Sachin Tendulkar. At the close of play I walked off slowly, acknowledging the ovation from the crease to the pavilion gate and then up the steps and through the Long Room, which was dark and cool. For one brief beautiful moment it felt as though Lord's belonged only to me.

I know, better than some, why you have to make the absolute most of something like that.

MY MUM HAS always urged me to go after whatever opportunities life offers. Along the way, I've always tried to make as many of my own as I can too. I've done so positively and with a wholehearted intensity. I never wanted to look back in old or even middle age and see a host of things – off the pitch as well as on it – that I could have done but didn't, missing out because I'd stayed away or held myself back or hadn't worked hard enough. Told I can't – rather than won't – achieve something, my first reaction is always to ask: 'Why not?'

And I've never needed reminding that you have to wring and squeeze every drop out of living. But I got a reminder anyway, and it devastated me.

In April 2016 James Taylor almost died.

It's one of those stories that you instantly doubt the accuracy of because it seems so improbable. I told myself it couldn't possibly be true. Surely some mistake had been made. Surely it had happened to someone else. A different James Taylor, completely unknown to me, must be sick and their identities had got confused or mixed up. Even when the sequence of events was laid out for me, the facts becoming irrefutable, I didn't want to believe them and I struggled to take them in. He'd been preparing for a pre-season match for Notts at Cambridge University. He'd been warming up – only routine, normal stuff – when his heart began to heave abnormally. In the dressing room he began to sweat profusely and needed oxygen. Taken back to Trent Bridge, he'd collapsed at the foot of some stairs. In hospital, the doctors found his heart thumping at 265 beats per minute. The normal resting rate for adults is between 60 to 100 beats per minute. The condition is called arrhythmogenic right ventricular cardiomyopathy. It's a mouthful to pronounce but it essentially means the rhythm and pumping mechanism of the heart is dangerously faulty.

This was Titch, my dear, dear friend. He was saved only because the doctors were able to implant a defibrillator into his heart.

I had thought Titch was as physically fit – super-fit, in fact – as anyone I'd ever known. I had assumed that we'd play beside or against one another for the next ten years and more. When the shock wore off, I remember crying. Out of relief and gratitude, just thankful that he was alive. Out of what I saw as the cruelty of it all, the fickleness and apparent randomness of fate. Titch was one of our best and brightest, several quarts of talent in a pint pot. He's also four months younger than I am. As if I wasn't already aware of it, here was another sign that the future – even tomorrow or next week – can have a habit of not quite turning out the way you expect it. Further proof, too, that sometimes what you consider as yours can be snatched away suddenly and without warning, becoming irrecoverably lost. His career was blossoming one moment and over the next.

I'm wary of the words 'tragedy' or 'tragic'. They creep frequently into reports about sport, attached to defeats or to describe failures that are really never more than stumbles or setbacks. Such indiscriminate overuse debases the genuine, deep meaning of those words. I don't even like to read 'tragedy' or 'tragic' in relation to my own story, though I've seen

them appear regularly enough in newspaper headlines about my past. For I think what really counts is always the present. What you make of it. How you respond to the hand you're dealt. Titch has shown me that again. He's fought back, demonstrating a courage most of us would like to possess but don't. The doctors originally told him not to exercise. Now he's a golf-course bandit, his talent already outstripping the generous club handicap he's been given. And the lesson he passes on every day is something I first learnt after my dad died nearly 20 years ago.

Life goes on. It must.

And you have to catch happiness as it flies, enjoying it there and then and for however long it lasts.

AFTERWORD

I AM BLUEY

3 January 2017, Leeds

SO A YEAR has passed.

I see some of it in the same way you recall a landscape as it rushes by from the window of a speeding train. It's blurry, indistinct. But what matters stands out and comes back bright and gleaming to me, as though the images are only a day old rather than 12 months.

My kit and my bags are already sorted and stacked. My departure for the start of another one-day series is imminent, the carousel of modern cricket always turning. Outside the sun is buried behind an ugly swell of clouds, almost as black as fresh bruising, that look full of rain. The wind is getting up too, dragging the cold with it from somewhere further north. Today, though, I'm thinking of another sky, which is clear blue, and a warmer climate in a different country. In my mind, at least, I'm 8,500 miles away. In Cape Town. Below Table Mountain, that great cathedral of rock. Batting at Newlands, which is still spotless and immaculately green, and where I feel the crowd is rooting for me. On the scoreboard, I'm on 99 again, patiently waiting for the loose ball that will take me to that hundred.

Just one more run ...

I decide to search for and then post a photograph of the Test on Instagram. I want to mark the occasion, letting everyone know how much it meant and continues to mean. I trawl the internet and find an upright, loosely cropped picture that shows both Ben Stokes and me. The shot is plain, without much movement, let alone drama. You'd think one quick glance would be enough to take in everything it offers. There's certainly no emotion in it – not even the merest flicker. Stokesy and I are walking together down a flight of stone steps. The low concrete supports of the pavilion are above us. There is a small knot of spectators leaning against a rail, the metal obscured by an advertising banner that you can't quite read. One of the spectators is already applauding and another is holding up his phone, about to snatch a close-up, side-on portrait of me in which I won't be smiling. I look rather sombre, like someone who's been dispatched to deliver bad news, and Stokesy, only a pace behind me, is the same. His head is bowed. His expression, completely blank, gives nothing away. I am carrying my bat, but we've both left our helmets and gloves on the outfield, where the sun will dry away the sweat in them.

Without a caption beneath it, I doubt anyone who wasn't there will look at either the background or our faces and identify the moment without a good deal of thought first. They won't necessarily register either what Stokesy and I have done or are about to do. You would only know that this is a hot afternoon somewhere because there are heavy, dwarf shadows, so the sun is clearly full and can't have travelled far from its noonday peak.

The photograph, taken at lunch on the second day at Newlands, reminds me of the morning session just gone – a blistering show of 196 runs in 25 overs – and what's to come. Not only in a couple of hours, but also for the rest of that South African tour, and then the summer and winter ahead. Hindsight infuses it with a personal significance that wouldn't otherwise be there. It captures me on the brink of something. I stare at it knowing what happens next. The message I post alongside the photograph is uncomplicated:

'A year ago today. A morning and a day I'll never forget!'

I don't exaggerate. I will *never* forget it. I will never forget the delivery from Stiaan van Zyl and the shot I played to it.

I will never forget the din of the ovation as the ball scuttled off to the boundary. I will never forget hearing afterwards how, for ten minutes while that final run continued to elude me, my mum and Becky barely moved, barely spoke and barely even breathed in their seats. At the end of the day's play, they were interviewed on *Test Match Special*, a collector's item because neither of them rarely discusses anything publicly, preferring to remain in the background. My mum was asked about how I'd looked skywards for an age after reaching my century, as though searching for a sign in it. She said the gesture was for my grandpa as well as my dad, which would have constituted breaking news to anyone who isn't a friend or part of our family.

My grandpa's death is so recent that I find it difficult to talk about him. It hurts too much. I can talk about my dad's at last only because such a great span of time has passed. I've learnt to accept his suicide even though a small part of me is still working out explanations for it – something minor that was missed or overlooked. Perhaps I always will.

IN TWO DAYS' time it'll be the anniversary of my dad's death. Again.

Of course, he's never far from my thoughts no matter where I am or what I'm doing. A place, a game, an incident somewhere or an unexpected word from someone can trigger a memory, which then triggers another, and suddenly I'm thinking about him, if only for a minute or two. But for this book I've been going over the last 20 years in the way you might slowly turn the pages of a family album, finding in it photos, cuttings and mementos that you'd either half-forgotten or didn't know you had. I've been putting the past and my reactions to it in order, I suppose, and I've also been giving them some shape. Sorting out the way things were. Dwelling on what I've made of them. Working out the life lessons. Wondering whether sharing what I've experienced can help or inspire or simply be a small comfort to anyone else. I hope it will be.

I've learnt – and this pleases me – that my dad's cricketing life and my own will always be intertwined, each illuminating the other, even though I will finish far behind the number of appearances he made for Yorkshire and also his length of service at Headingley. I've learnt to speak about him in the past tense even though he's preserved in my memory exactly as he used to be to me: hale and hearty and smiling. I've learnt that it's possible to recover – and prosper – from awful loss even though you go on missing and loving those who have gone. I've learnt how adversity and suffering can build character and I know that you can become stronger in some of the broken places because of it – even though I wouldn't prescribe the experience to anyone.

I was only ever briefly angry with my dad for leaving us.

It happened shortly after his death, when things were at their darkest and the grief in me was raw and at its worst. The feeling came and went again, wiped away because I realised he loved us, and I realised, too, how desperate he must have been to make the choice he did. But I've never had to forgive my dad because I've never believed there was anything to forgive him for in the first place.

I do, nevertheless, think about what my dad's death denied us. All the matches, as an honoured guest, that he could have watched me play in. All the birthday parties, all the holidays and all the Christmases he's missed with my mum and Becky and me. All the family photos in which he doesn't appear. I learnt, as I grew older, that my dad wondered how different his life would have been if he'd met my mum sooner. In the same way I've thought about the times the two of us could have shared, the stories he could have told me and the advice he could have given. I never got to buy him a pint. He never got to buy me one. At least I can still recall his voice, the acoustic accompaniment to some of the memories I have of him.

As a family we have small keepsakes of him too. There's the round-faced watch he wore, a combination of gold and silver. There's a piece of coral from the Caribbean Sea, which he attached to a gold link chain that he almost never took off. And I have something of him that belongs only to me. It's his nickname. When I came into the Yorkshire academy I was christened Bluey almost immediately. You never get to choose your nickname and you're always stuck with whatever you've been given once it becomes estab- lished. At first I recoiled a little uneasily from it. I'd heard so many people call my dad Bluey. Even those who knew him only by reputation would refer to him that way, as though he was their pal. Bluey was his; it seemed to me that the copyright on the nickname belonged solely to him. I didn't think I had any right to it. Absurd as this may sound, I also felt in the beginning as though I needed his permission to use it.

Now I think my dad would be chuffed to find out that the small boy he knew is Bluey too.

I'VE BEEN THINKING about my dad's relationship with Yorkshire.

I've read – and had it said to me – that the club treated him shabbily before he finally left them and then again after he'd gone. There was a reason for that, I think. He'd been so candid and so public about his criticism of the internal politics there, which he loathed. 'Committees don't win cricket matches,' he'd say. 'They just make it harder for the players.' My dad knew he was right, but being proved so never offered cast-iron protection against the agendas and self-interest of others. He had plenty of friends at Yorkshire, but not enough of them were in high places to offer practical as well as moral support.

I have to stress, very strongly, that the Yorkshire of now is far different from the Yorkshire of then. Like my dad, I can't imagine wanting to play for anyone else. I am a Yorkshireman, and I care about Yorkshire as much as he did. Today there's an established policy of inviting back former players, making them feel that Headingley is still home. What every one of them achieved for the county is respected and counts for something. From what I can surmise, based on the evidence of what happened to my dad and also to a few others, this wasn't necessarily the case a quarter of a century ago.

For the last five years of his life my dad seldom stepped back into Headingley. He felt effectively banished from it shortly after his retirement. The schism that opened up between him and the county was emphasised when my half-brother Andrew, making his debut for Derbyshire, faced Yorkshire at Chesterfield. We went as a family. My dad put on a flat cap and watched from behind a tree in an attempt not to be noticed. But he wouldn't go near the Yorkshire dressing room, telling my uncle Ted: 'If they don't want me, I don't want to be there.'

The event that precipitated this was a lunch held in the red-brick building that was once the Headingley pavilion. Two things happened during it, each connected to the other and both petty and ridiculous. My dad declined to wear a name badge because he thought the thick pin would damage the lapel of his light suit. He also felt that everyone in the room would have a reasonably fair idea of his identity without it. You were supposed to 'reserve' a place by eventually dropping the badge on to the table. My dad, unaware of this, thought he'd already claimed his and my mum's seats until he found someone else sitting in one of them. There followed a short round of musical chairs before he ended up on the balcony.

A day or so later Yorkshire sent my dad a letter, alleging that he'd been rude and abusive to an official. Only an apology would get him officially into Headingley again. Otherwise he was 'no longer welcome there'. My dad felt he'd been unjustly wronged. He put his foot down on a point of principle and refused to move it. I don't want to idealise him; I know he had his faults. But the idea that Yorkshire would write to him, rather than speak face to face, infuriated him.

When my dad spoke to someone, he always preferred to look them in the eye. Nor was he the sort of man to whisper his views behind a hand. If something was on his mind – especially a grievance or a passionate belief – he told you about it without necessarily calculating the full consequences first. He thought these could be smoothed out later on. He could give an ear-bashing to a player or a reporter, but everything would usually be forgiven and forgotten within 48 hours, the slate wiped scrupulously clean as far as he was concerned. Any player who incurred his displeasure would be told in the dressing room, and any reporter would often find my dad marching into a press box to debate a nuanced point. On one occasion he confronted a correspondent without noticing that another, merely an innocent bystander, was so scared of being struck by shrapnel from the ensuing rumpus that he cowed in a phone cubicle until the whole thing blew itself out. My dad was convinced that no grievance, no problem and certainly no difference of opinion couldn't be solved if you sat down together and supped a pint or three until last orders was called.

So, while I'm aware that he wasn't always as tactful as he might have been in private places, such as the dressing room or the press box, I also know he didn't resort to salty exchanges during public suit-and-tie affairs, especially when women were present. After that Headingley function, he insisted that there was absolutely nothing to apologise for. My mum agreed with him. So an impasse began – and so an impasse persisted.

No one in life is immune from change, but his connection with Yorkshire cricket had elated and sustained my dad for so long that, while not playing for them was bad enough, being made unwelcome at Headingley proved crushing for him. He didn't feel as though he could walk through the front gate anymore. He brooded over a possible ulterior motive behind the complaint made against him and the ultimatum accompanying it. Since he was thinking of putting himself forward for the committee, he saw the charge as fabricated: a convenient and none too elaborate smokescreen behind which he could be hustled out of the way. His anger intensified and his position became more entrenched because of it. I think he never quite got over the way Yorkshire treated him then.

Some will join the dots too predictably, connecting my dad's death primarily to his estrangement from cricket. There's even a theory that cricketers are more susceptible than most to melancholia, depression and suicide both during their careers and afterwards. The evidence offered in support includes the suicide of figures such as AE Stoddart, Albert Trott and Arthur Shrewsbury, who each shot themselves, and Harold Gimblett and RC Robertson-Glasgow, who both took overdoses. I don't agree. As I see it, playing cricket doesn't make you vulnerable to mental illness any more than I imagine other jobs do – from digging a ditch to driving a lorry or working nine to five in an office.

'It's a great life,' my dad once said of Yorkshire cricket. I'm aware that without it, and the familiar rhythm and routines of the summer, he was restless and out of sorts in the beginning. But cricket wasn't responsible for his death. In the end he was worried only about my mum's cancer, how he would cope if she died and also the financial future of his business. There's an awful irony about the latter. Only two weeks after his death, the company was asked to take on a big order that would have guaranteed a considerable income.

I wish he'd known that. I wish he'd been aware that there was the promise of so much more ahead for him.

MY DAD PLAYED his last game for Yorkshire in a place where he belonged: his beloved Scarborough. There were nearly 9,000 at North Marine Road to watch him in a 50-over Festival Trophy match against Essex. In early September sunshine, he was applauded all the way to the crease and then back to the pavilion after making 36 in a run-chase, the crowd's allegiance with him for every shot, every familiar shout of 'wait on' or 'running one' or 'not coming'. My mum was there to watch him. She was pregnant with Becky and she held me – then almost one year old – in her arms. When my dad's innings was over, his career done, he doffed his cap towards all corners and gave a little bow each time, like a performer disappearing into the wings of a stage, the curtain swishing around him before it closes. In their obituary *Wisden* described him as 'perhaps the only unequivocally popular man in Yorkshire'. It was certainly true on that day and on that ground.

After my dad died, there was only one place to scatter his ashes.

My mum and Uncle Ted took them to North Marine Road, where Scarborough Cricket Club's memorial garden is a small patch of greenery not far from the pavilion and between two stands. A plaque, bearing in plain lettering his name and the dates of his birth and death, is affixed nearby. Every time I go there, I visit the spot before the main gates have opened or after the ground has emptied. I have what I call 'a moment' with him there. When my mum and Uncle Ted took the lid off the urn, letting the ashes run out, a rush of wind got up from nowhere. The ashes blew back towards them. 'He wants to have the final word,' Uncle Ted said.

Perhaps we should have expected that.

My dad's memorial service had already been staged in Ripon Cathedral, the stone of its twin towers rising over the market town. The view across the Perpendicular nave, from the north aisle towards the south, is spectacular – the arches high-pointed, asymmetrical and Romanesque. More than 600 people were there, listening to the speeches, hearing the soft notes of the cathedral organ, remembering the past. It was here that my dad's colleague Phil Carrick used the phrase that's been borrowed often to describe him: 'He wasn't a great batsman. Maybe he wasn't a great wicket-keeper. But he was a great cricketer.'

In diffused light, amid all the architectural beauty, Uncle Ted was the last to speak, a formal goodbye from his best friend, which we thought was most fitting.

Television cameras had filmed some of what had gone before, but the paraphernalia of outside broadcasting – arc lights, cables, sound equipment – was being packed away as Uncle Ted cleared his throat and arranged his notes. He was about to say of my dad: 'If ever there was a greater character and friend, I have yet to meet him.' But the words 'David Leslie Bairstow', the introduction to a farewell crammed full of their shared experiences, had barely left his lips when a crashing gust of wind – far stronger than the one at Scarborough – battered the side of the building and brought with it a thick splattering of rain. The sudden rush of the wind rattled the stained-glass windows, almost shaking them out of their ancient frames, before swirling right through the big oak doors, as if flinging them apart, and then filling the whole cathedral. The wind blasted down the aisle and up towards the vaulting of the ceiling in a mighty whoosh that echoed afterwards. It was fleeting, coming and going in scarcely a minute but creating something that seemed extraordinary and freaky.

Uncle Ted had no option. He had to pause, waiting for it to pass. From the wooden lectern he looked down at my mum and at Becky and me. We were sitting in the front row, almost directly in front of him. Uncle Ted stared at my mum. Each had the same thought, flashing instantly into their mind. No other explanation seemed possible to them. My mum looked back at Uncle Ted, smiled and silently mouthed the words:

'He's here.'

In truth, of course, my dad's always here. He's here whenever and wherever I play because so many spectators look at me but also remember watching him. He's here when he's mentioned in relation to what I've done, or he's recalled on the radio or on TV. He's here again when, together as a family, we go over the quirky stories about him, told umpteen times before but which we'll never tire of. He's here when I meet one of his former teammates. He's here – as large as he ever was – whenever someone I've never seen before approaches me and shares some nugget of news about him that I didn't know. If you got out a map of any cricket-playing country in the world and jabbed the point of a compass into it at random, I'm sure you'd find at least several dozen blokes who considered him to be a friend. In Australia I got stopped by an ex-rugby-league pro, who presented me with one of my dad's testimonial ties. 'Here,' he said. 'I think it's about time this came back to you.' He explained how he and my dad had met at Headingley one night and struck up a conversation that lasted until the wee small hours – and beyond. 'Your dad,' he said, 'was a decent bloke.'

That decent bloke lives on. In our memory, of course, but also in the memory of so many others. He lives on in photographs you'll find on the walls of cricket clubs. He lives on because his name is on an honours board somewhere. He lives on in cricket's history and in thick statistical records. He lives on in newspaper and magazine archives. Most of all, I hope, he lives in the book you're holding; for that is the point of it.

One day I want to re-create the same kind of home in the same kind of environment that we all shared in Marton cum Grafton. I want to emulate that lifestyle. I'd like it to be out in gentle hilly country. I'd like to have a wide garden surrounded by open fields that slide into the far, far distance. Somewhere that makes the sky seem high and broad. Somewhere there are dry-stone walls and hedges and clumps of plump trees. Somewhere wildlife is a neighbour, and the air is clean and you know the time of year from the way the crops are growing, the flowers that are in bloom or from the type of birds that have arrived. Somewhere I can have dogs, possibly another pair of Rhodesian ridgebacks. I'd like to go for walks, whatever the weather. I'd like to have barbecues. And I'd like to build a wooden veranda and sit contemplatively on it, just as my dad did.

He'll be there. He always is.

ACKNOWLEDGEMENTS

LIKE NEARLY EVERYTHING I do, this book has been a family affair.

I wouldn't have gone ahead with it without the support, as ever, of Mum and Becky. Becky, so used to listening to me talk about cricket, gave only one instruction: 'Don't just go on about saving byes – you'll bore the pants off people.' She was right, of course.

What she and Mum mean to me is captured in the title of the prologue. Everything is for them and because of them. It always will be. I promise.

I'm lucky. You can't choose your extended family, but I know I've been blessed with an outstanding one – loving and caring and kindly. You'll appreciate after reading the previous 300 pages how much my maternal grandparents have influenced me. I still feel the loss of my beloved grandpa. I still cherish my grandma.

I also want to thank the two Andrews – my mum's brother and my half-brother – for their role in our lives over the past 20-odd years. And as for Uncle Ted … well, he is family too. We'd do anything for him because, ever present, he has always done everything for us.

They say you should always keep a friendship in constant repair. My friend Gareth and I have done so ever since we first met as schoolboys. He's what a best mate should be.

Confronting the past can be a daunting business – especially in these circumstances – so I'm also very grateful to my co-author, Duncan, for making the process as painless as he possibly could for me. He asks that others searching for a co-author form an orderly queue!

A Clear Blue Sky – and how I can still see it above me at Newlands – is really my last word on Dad. I'm sure, despite its publication, that someone, somewhere will still ask me how he is and that someone, somewhere else will still call me David. But at least I can point them towards a copy of this book, which is, I hope, a fitting tribute to Dad and a public, loving thank you in paper and ink to Mum and Becky.

Jonny Bairstow, *Leeds, August 2017*